THE
TENDER

WARRIOR

THE LIFE OF DAVID
VOLUME I
1 SAMUEL 8–29

DR. DAVID JEREMIAH

with Dr. David Jeremiah

CONTENTS

ABOUT
DR. DAVID JEREMIAH
AND TURNING POINT

D r. David Jeremiah is the founder of Turning Point, a ministry committed to providing Christians with sound Bible teaching relevant to today's changing times through radio and television broadcasts, audio series, and books. Dr. Jeremiah's "common-sense" teaching on topics such as family, stress, the New Age, angels, and biblical prophecy forms the foundation of Turning Point.

David and his wife Donna reside in El Cajon, California, where he is the senior pastor of Shadow Mountain Community Church and chancellor of Christian Heritage College. David and Donna have four children and four grandchildren.

In 1982, Dr. Jeremiah brought the same solid teaching to San Diego television that he shares weekly with his congregation. Shortly thereafter, Turning Point expanded its ministry to radio. Dr. Jeremiah's inspiring messages can now be heard on radio and television nationally and internationally.

Because Dr. Jeremiah desires to know his listening audience, he travels nationwide holding "A Night of Encouragement" ministry rallies and Spiritual Enrichment conferences that touch the hearts and lives of many. According to Dr. Jeremiah, "At some point in time, everyone reaches a turning point, and for every person that moment is unique, an experience to hold onto forever. There's so much changing in today's world that sometimes it's difficult to choose the right path. Turning Point offers people an understanding of God's Word, as well as the opportunity to make a difference in their lives."

Dr. Jeremiah has authored numerous books, including *Escape the Coming Night* (Revelation), *The Handwriting on the Wall* (Daniel), *Invasion of Other Gods* (New Age), *Overcoming Loneliness, What the Bible Says About Angels, The Power of Encouragement, Prayer—The Great Adventure, God in You* (Holy Spirit), *Gifts from God* (Parenting), *Jesus' Final Warning, A Bend in the Road, Slaying the Giants in Your Life, My Heart's Desire, Sanctuary, The Things That Matter,* and *Life Wide Open.*

ABOUT THIS
STUDY GUIDE

The purpose of this Turning Point study guide is to reinforce Dr. David Jeremiah's dynamic, in-depth teaching and to aid the reader in applying biblical truth to his or her daily life. This study guide is designed to be used in conjunction with Dr. Jeremiah's *The Tender Warrior: The Life of David* audio series, but it may be used by itself for personal or group Bible study.

STRUCTURE OF THE LESSONS

Each lesson is based on one of the messages in *The Tender Warrior: The Life of David* audiocassette or compact disc series and focuses on specific passages in the Bible. Each lesson is composed of the following elements:

- *Outline*

The outline at the beginning of the lesson gives a clear, concise picture of the passage being studied and provides a helpful framework for readers as they listen to Dr. Jeremiah's teaching.

- *Overview*

The overview summarizes Dr. Jeremiah's teaching on the passage being studied in the lesson. Readers should refer to the biblical passages in their own Bibles as they study the overview.

- *Application*

This section contains a variety of questions designed to help readers dig deeper into the lesson and the Scriptures, and to apply the lesson to their daily lives. For Bible study groups or Sunday school classes, these questions will provide a springboard for group discussion and interaction.

- *Did You Know?*

This section presents a fascinating fact, historical note, or insight that adds a point of interest to the preceding lesson.

USING THIS GUIDE FOR GROUP STUDY

The lessons in this study guide are suitable for Sunday school classes, small-group studies, elective Bible studies, or home Bible study groups. Each person in the group should have his or her own study guide.

When possible, the study guide should be used with the corresponding tape or compact disc series. You may wish to assign the study guide as homework prior to the meeting of the group and then use the meeting time to listen to the message and discuss the lesson.

FOR CONTINUING STUDY

A complete catalog of Dr. Jeremiah's materials for personal and group study is available through Turning Point. To obtain a catalog, additional study guides, or more information about Turning Point, call 1-800-947-1993 or write to: Turning Point, P.O. Box 3838, San Diego, CA 92163.

Dr. Jeremiah's *Turning Point* program is currently heard or viewed around the world on radio, television, and the Internet in English. *Momento Decisivo,* the Spanish translation of Dr. Jeremiah's messages, can be heard on radio in every Spanish speaking country in the world. In some areas the television broadcast provides Arabic subtitles.

Contact Turning Point for radio and television program times and stations in your area. Or visit our website at www.turningpointonline.org.

THE TENDER WARRIOR: THE LIFE OF DAVID

VOLUME 1

INTRODUCTION

W hen you hear the name "David," what do you think of? The boy who killed Goliath? The shepherd who wrote Psalm 23? The king who fell into sin with Bathsheba?

David was all those things, but he was much more. He was a tender-hearted man who cared for his parents and watched carefully over the sheep left in his care. He was a warrior who led his men into battle and became known for his courage and bravery. He was a natural leader who charmed people with his charisma and was loved by a nation. He was a man who struggled with lying and depression, and who resorted to deception when he should have relied on his faith in God.

There is no one picture that sums up David's life, for like all men, he was complex. The poems he left behind reveal a man who loved God and wanted the Lord's will to be done. God once called him "a man after His own heart" (1 Samuel 13:14). David was truly a tender warrior—combining the care of the shepherd with the toughness of a soldier.

The life of David appeals to every man and woman because we can all identify with his struggles. Each of us has had to face big battles, jealous friends, and unexpected temptations. David saw public successes, but it seemed to be followed by personal mistakes. He knew both exhilaration and discouragement, victory and defeat. Throughout it all, he maintained a heart for God.

Perhaps the reason people love David so much is because he opened up his life and allowed others to know his feelings. His psalms are filled with words both joyous and dejected, glad-hearted and sad-spirited. He sang songs of tender love, and songs of terrible wrath. Everyone can see their own life reflected in the life of David. That's why we love his story.

In these twelve lessons, we will explore the victory over Goliath and the high cost David paid for his success. We will see how he treated people, look at his mistakes, and examine his darkest days.

The story of David is largely the story of Saul, for it was the disobedience and rejection of that king that led directly to the anointing of a shepherd king. David, like all of us, was an ordinary person, thrust into an extraordinary situation. A lowly shepherd, he was called by God to become king over Israel. He was a tender warrior, and this study of his life will help you to see him in a new light.

INTRODUCTION TO DAVID

1 Samuel 8–15

In this lesson we will learn what
sets a great man apart from other men—
from one of the greatest men who ever lived.

OUTLINE

King David was one of the greatest men to ever walk the face of this earth. As we begin our study of his life, we must first look at what made David great.

   I. **David Was Great Because of His Context**
     A. The Context of His Life Historically
     B. The Context of His Life Personally
     C. The Context of His Life Biblically

  II. **David Was Great Because of His Charisma**
     A. David Was a Man of Physical Charisma
     B. David Was a Man of Personal Charisma
     C. David Was a Man of National Charisma

 III. **David Was Great Because of His Creativity**

 IV. **David Was Great Because of the Choice of His Life**

  V. **David Was Great Because of the Confession of His Life**

When Jesse and his wife had a son, they gave him a unique name: David, which literally means "beloved." I think that tells us a great deal about the parents. They already had seven boys; but when their eighth son was born, they called him their beloved. Though it was a unique name in that day, it has now become a common name. Nearly everyone knows or is related to someone named David. But it is not an overstatement to say that the uniqueness of David's name is symbolic of the uniqueness of his person. He was the central figure of the Old Testament and one of the greatest men who ever lived. As we begin a study of David, we must first consider some of the reasons for his greatness.

DAVID WAS GREAT BECAUSE OF HIS CONTEXT

David was a great man because of the time in which he lived. Some people are born to greatness because they are born at just the right time. I doubt we would know as much about Abraham Lincoln had he not been born during the great controversy over slavery. The context of the times allowed Lincoln to use his leadership to emancipate the slaves.

By the same token, we probably would not know as much about Martin Luther King, had he not been born in a time of racial turbulence. The context of the times allowed his leadership to arise during a tremendous time of revolution in our country. Often the greatness of an individual is predicated upon the context of his life. With that in mind, consider the context of David's life.

The Context of His Life Historically

David was born for an important time in the history of his country. For five centuries before his birth, the nation of Israel had been in decline. The last great leader to have led the nation was Joshua, and the book of Judges tells us that after Joshua and the elders of his generation died, there grew up a generation that did not know the Lord, or any of His works. Thus the nation of Israel went into decline. Vicious oppressors rose up to torment the nation, and hunger and famine made her a country constantly in distress. Whenever the suffering grew great, the people would cry out to God; and He would raise up a judge or deliverer to help them out of their predicament. Sometimes these judges were good men like Gideon or Samuel, other times they were unstable men like Samson. But God continued providing leaders to Israel to deliver them from their troubles.

Samuel was the last of the judges, and during his reign the people revolted against God. They were tired of having judges, and looking around at the other nations, they determined that they needed a king. So in 1 Samuel 8:5, the people came to Samuel and said, "Make us a king to judge us like all the nations." These words displeased Samuel, but when he prayed to God, the Lord answered by saying, "Hearken unto the voice of the people in all that they say unto thee: for they have not rejected thee, but they have rejected Me, that I should not reign over them" (1 Samuel 8:7). So the people got their king.

The next few chapters tell about the anointing of King Saul, the man God chose to be king over Israel. He was a man who was "a choice young man, and a goodly: and there was not among the children of Israel a goodlier person than he: from his shoulders upward he was higher than any of the people" (9:2). So Saul, a big and good-looking physical specimen, was chosen because he *looked* like a king. He had all the makings of becoming a national hero. Unfortunately, though his reign started out well, it was short and disappointing.

Saul took for himself the roles of prophet and priest, even offering sacrifices to God though it was not his responsibility to do so. Once, when God told Saul to obliterate a nation, Saul decided not to fully obey, then lied to the prophet Samuel about his lack of obedience. Finally God had had enough. He sent this message to Saul through His prophet: "Rebellion is as the sin of witchcraft, and stubbornness is as iniquity and idolatry. Because you have rejected the word of the Lord, He also has rejected you from being king" (1 Samuel 15:23 NKJ). The Bible says that the Lord repented that He had ever made Saul king, and he told His prophet where to find the new king.

That's the historical context of David's birth. After five centuries of decline, and a wicked king who refused to honor God, the nation was in dire need of real leadership. The Old Testament shows that whenever Israel was in need of a leader, the Lord provided the right man. When they needed Moses, God raised up Moses. When they needed a judge, He raised up a judge. Now that they needed a godly king, the Lord had prepared a shepherd boy to take the place of leadership over the nation. David came to the position just when his country needed him.

The Context of His Life Personally

Have you ever wondered what sort of family produces a leader like David? As we explore his background, we find that his family was not wealthy. There is no evidence his father had any servants. When first introduced to David, he is out tending the sheep, a job usually given to the household servants. And when Jesse sent a gift to King Saul, it was something simple, not the gift of a wealthy man. It is also evident that David did not hold a place of esteem in the family, from the way others in the family treated him. When Samuel came looking for the man who would be king, he first looked over Jesse's other sons, and had to ask the father, "Is there anyone else?" Jesse hadn't even thought to bring his youngest son—David was an afterthought by his father.

Though David wasn't important in his own family, it's interesting to see that he always treated his family well. He was tender toward both his mother and father, once even asking the king of Moab to protect them because he feared King Saul would try and hurt them.

When David was in exile, running from Saul and hiding in caves with his band of renegades around him, he spoke longingly of his home. He said that he would love to have a refreshing drink of water from the well at Bethlehem, from which he used to drink as a boy. Three of the brave men close by took it as a challenge, fought through the enemy lines, and brought back cool water for David. His home life had been important to him, and his family was always treasured.

The Context of His Life Biblically

David is a very important person in the total context of Scripture. He is mentioned in the New Testament more than any other Old Testament character. His name comes up 16 times in Matthew, 13 times in Luke, 11 times in Acts, 7 times in Mark, 3 times in Romans and Revelation, 2 times in John and Hebrews, and 1 time in 2 Timothy. His is perhaps the most complete biography in the Bible outside of Jesus Christ. Sixty-two chapters in the Word of God are devoted to his story. David is a man of greatness because of the context of his life historically, personally, and biblically.

David Was Great Because of His Charisma

David was charismatic in the biblical sense of the word. People were drawn to him because of his personality. There are several aspects of his charisma that are clear in Scripture.

David Was a Man of Physical Charisma

Apparently David was not a big man. His brother Eliab was much bigger than he was. But David was strong and athletic. He had quick feet, so that he could jump over walls and outrun an enemy army. He was also strong, so that he could break an iron bar and fling stones with deadly force. He was too small to get into Saul's armor, but was powerful enough to kill a bear and a lion with his own hands.

First Samuel 16:12 describes David as being "ruddy, and withal of a beautiful countenance, and goodly to look to." The Hebrew words literally mean he had large, liquid eyes, with a good complexion. He must have been a real charmer. Many scholars believe that David was blessed with beautiful hair, either golden or reddish in color, and it set him apart from his Jewish family. When people looked at David, there was something striking about him. In verse 18, a servant describes him as "cunning in playing, and a mighty valiant man, and a man of war, and prudent in matters, and a comely person, and the Lord is with him." David certainly had a physical charisma.

David Was a Man of Personal Charisma

David is the one guy in the Bible with whom nearly everyone can identify. His life has many similarities to our own lives. The Scriptures record him going from one difficulty into the next—sometimes so quickly you can't catch your breath! He is in exile one moment, and the next moment he is king. He is gently playing his harp one minute, and the next minute he is a warrior in battle. The magnetism of his personality is captivating. He charged Goliath with youthful, daring courage, led a band of outlaws with wisdom, and defeated armies with his military acumen.

David was also admired by women. After he killed Goliath, the ladies made up a song about him that became number one on Israel's hit parade. He simply captured the hearts of his people. He was a young, attractive, athletic, creative man, who showed himself to be courageous for his country and devoted to his parents. People were drawn to him. Michal, the daughter of Saul, fell in love with him. Jonathan, the son of Saul, became David's best friend. The king of the Philistines once said, "Thou art good in my sight, as an angel of God." David exuded a personal charisma that made people love him.

David Was a Man of National Charisma

First Samuel 18:16 best describes the attitude of Israel toward David: "All Israel and Judah loved David, because he went out and came in before them." He embodied the entire life of Israel. He stood for everything the Jews believed was important. As a shepherd, he represented the working class. As a soldier, he represented the warriors who protected the nation. As a king, he represented leadership with the nation. As a musician, his songs spoke for the nation. As a poet, he became his country's poet laureate, revealing their thoughts and walk with God. The people of Israel loved him because they identified with him. God gifted him with great ability to draw people toward him.

DAVID WAS GREAT BECAUSE OF HIS CREATIVITY

God gave David tremendous powers of creativity. He was a most unusual person, incorporating both the strength of a warrior and athlete with the gentleness of a poet and singer.

David wrote both strong and gentle songs. Seventy-three of the psalms in our hymnbook in the Bible were written by him. As a matter of fact, our modern practice of singing hymns began with David. Before David, songs were occasionally written to celebrate significant events like Israel's defeat of the Egyptian army, but nobody displayed the depth and creativity of David. When we read the Psalms, we find a creative genius.

Have you ever been so caught up in God's beauty that you wished for the gift of a poet, so that you could describe the scene in word pictures? David had that gift. His hymns of praise offer wonderful pictures of God. His words of pain are filled with descriptive phrases from his own discouragement and depression. All of his psalms reveal his personal walk with God. Occasionally I'll hear someone suggest we shouldn't have music of personal testimony; but if that were true, we'd have to throw out much of

David's writing, for his songs are filled with words of both praise and pain. He was a gifted, creative man.

DAVID WAS GREAT BECAUSE OF THE CHOICE OF HIS LIFE

There are five passages which tell us how David became king over Israel, and they all reveal one thing: God chose David. The Lord was fed up with King Saul, and chose to make David king. In 1 Samuel 13:14 we are told the Lord sought David. In Psalm 89:20 we read the Lord found David. In Psalm 78:70 we see the Lord chose David. In 1 Samuel 13:14 are the words, "The Lord has commanded him." And in 1 Samuel 16:1, the Bible says that the Lord has provided David. Everything that happened in making David king was due to the hand of God.

There was a moment of transition for Israel. First Samuel 16:13–14 reveals that the Spirit of the Lord departed from Saul, and that Spirit came to rest upon the heart of David. The number one reason for his greatness was that God chose him. The Lord's sovereign hand was upon him, whether he was in exile in a cave, or in majesty on the throne. When David stood before Goliath, God was with him. When he sat in the field and penned great hymns, God was with him. There is no other way to explain his greatness that to say that David was the choice of God.

DAVID WAS GREAT BECAUSE OF THE CONFESSION OF HIS LIFE

Finally, as we explore the person of David, we have to remember that his entire life is on display in the Old Testament. If he were to live today, the tabloids would only want to focus on his sin. They would say he was a great man, but he blew it, and cancel out the things God accomplished through him. Our culture seems better at telling how a man falls than describing the influence of his life.

As we read through the life of King David in the Bible, we see his failings, but in context with his greatness. His sin is a note of reality, for without that sin we would never be able to identify with him. His charm, creativity, and abilities would make him somehow untouchable. But David was a man who fell into sin like all the rest of us. The summary of his life can be found in 1 Kings 15:5: "David did that which was right in the eyes of the Lord, and had not turned aside from anything that he commanded him all the days of his life, save only in the matter of Uriah the Hittite."

God judges people differently than we do. We take a man's failure and make it his whole life. God takes a man's failure and makes it the exception to a life that is otherwise honorable.

The fact is, David was a frail man and he blew it, but he confessed his sin and moved on. And the Lord forgave him, remembering the overall impact of his life. God even referred to David as "a man after My own heart." Perhaps the secret of David's greatness was his confession. Willing to admit his failings, he allowed God to continue using him. The God of David is the God of the second chance. And He is our God, too, willing to forgive us and offer us another chance at greatness.

APPLICATION

1. Why is studying the life of David interesting to you?

   a. What do you already know about his life?

   b. What do those stories reveal about his character?

2. How can the context of history help shape a man?

   a. Would Abraham Lincoln have been as great a president in the early 1700s?

   b. How did the context of Israel at the time of David allow him to become a great king?

3. What do you think God was looking for in a king?

   a. Why would a shepherd from a poor family provide that leadership?

4. How does the life of David reveal his creativity?

    a. Why is it so hard for us to combine strength with gentleness, or a warrior with wisdom?

5. In the end, we see that David was great because God chose him for greatness. In what ways has God chosen you?

    a. To what types of activities or ministries has He called you?

DID YOU KNOW?

The genealogy of David is well attested in Scripture which is not surprising given his prominence in biblical history. A unique genealogy is found in Ruth 4:16–22. Ruth, the Moabite widow, married the prominent Israelite landowner, Boaz. Their son was Obed, whose son was Jesse, whose seventh son was David. So David's great-grandmother was Ruth, a non-Israelite. The book of Ruth forms a bridge between the tumultuous period of the Judges when Israel suffered greatly, and the more stable period of the kings, especially the kingship of David. Just as God restored Ruth's fortunes in life through her marriage to Boaz, so God restored Israel's fortunes through their son, David. And so God will restore the earth's fortunes through the Son of David, Jesus Christ (Matthew 1:1).

MAN APPOINTS, BUT GOD ANOINTS

1 Samuel 16:1–13

*In this lesson we will learn how
God selects His leaders.*

OUTLINE

The man God had selected to be the king of Israel wasn't at all what
the people had expected. But His way of choosing and preparing
people is different from our own way. Man appoints leaders, but
God anoints them.

I. **The Responsibility for Anointing Is God's**

II. **The Requirements for Anointing Are God's**
   A. Spiritual Attitude
   B. Servant Heart
   C. Private Person

III. **The Response to Anointing Is God's**

D avid was born at a time when leadership was in great demand. The judges had come to power and presided over a weak and wicked country, until the people pleaded with Samuel to appoint for them a king. The leadership of the king they received, Saul, began to fail. The nation was worsening. Yet all through this difficult time, God was at work. He had been searching, finding, choosing, and preparing David to be king of Israel. The Lord put His hand upon David and said, "This is my man."

As we study the Scriptures, we find that God has a definite way of making choices. In 1 Samuel 16, we see the difference between the way man functions and the way God functions. On the one hand, we have Saul—the choice of the people. On the other hand, we have David—the choice of God. The people appoint, but God anoints.

THE RESPONSIBILITY FOR ANOINTING IS GOD'S

Back in 1 Samuel 8, the leaders of the people had said, "Make us a king to judge us like all the nations." When Samuel heard those words, he wept, for he knew the people were out of line. God concurred with that assessment, for He told Samuel that in choosing a king, the people had rejected the Lord's leadership. Hosea the prophet, in commenting upon that situation, quotes God as saying, "I gave thee a king in Mine anger, and took him away in My wrath" (Hosea 13:11). It was as though the Lord said, "You want a king? Fine! Have one . . . but you'll be sorry."

The selection of Saul was initiated by man. The only reason Israel had a king was because of the human longing for leadership. God was not part of the decision, other than to grant the request made from the hardness of the people's hearts. He gave them exactly what they wanted.

But contrast that with the selection of David. His was a divine initiative. In 1 Samuel 16, God tells Samuel, "How long wilt thou mourn for Saul, seeing I have rejected him from reigning over Israel? . . . I have provided me a king." David was God's choice, and he would be God's king. It was the Lord who sent Samuel to find David, it was the Lord who promised to make His selection clear, and it was the Lord who said, "Thou shalt anoint unto Me him whom I name unto thee" (verse 3). When man chose, they selected a lousy king, whose kingdom and life ended in disaster. But when God chose, He selected the ideal king, whose kingdom and life reflected a heart for the Lord.

THE REQUIREMENTS FOR ANOINTING ARE GOD'S

In verse 6, we see that Samuel arrives at Jesse's house and starts looking for somebody who would make a good king. Remember, it was Samuel who had been responsible for bringing Saul, so Samuel probably thought he'd know the right man as soon as he saw him. As Jesse began to introduce Samuel to his sons, Samuel was immediately taken with the oldest boy, Eliab. The Bible tells us that Eliab was not unlike Saul, a big man with plenty of energy and great strength. As soon as Samuel saw him, he thought, "This must be the man!"

But Eliab was not the Lord's choice. Neither was the second son, Abinadab, nor Shammah, the third son. Jesse paraded all his sons before Samuel, but none of them were the right man for the job. You see, God was looking for something that could not be seen on the outside. He wasn't looking at stature or strength, but at the heart. The Lord said to Samuel, "Look not on his countenance, or on the height of his stature; because I have refused him: for the Lord seeth not as man seeth; for man looketh on the outward appearance, but the Lord looketh on the heart" (verse 7).

That is a crucial verse for our narcissistic age. Everybody in our culture is evaluating people on their outward appearances. We look for beauty, performance, and things we can visualize or investigate. Young people often select marriage partners on outward appearances, personnel offices select people on appearance and past performance. But God casts aside physical appearance, making His selection based on spiritual attitude.

Spiritual Attitude

The Scripture says that David was a man after God's own heart, so that whatever God wanted was exactly what David wanted. The purposes and priorities of the Lord were imprinted on his heart. That's the quality God was looking for in selecting a king for Israel.

I have found that in working with others, the heart is the best gauge. People can talk about their experience and accomplishments, but what I've found most helpful is to explore the person's heart. If I can find a person who wants what God wants, I'm confident that we'll work well together. In the house of Jesse, God ignored the outward appearance of the other boys and concentrated on the inward spiritual attitude of David.

Servant Heart

When the Lord describes David in Psalm 89:20, He calls him "David my servant." The Lord doesn't want someone strong in spirit, He wants someone who is a servant. Rather that somebody who will think about their own accomplishments, He wants someone who will think about the needs of others.

David has been a shepherd, caring for his sheep, and that was a quality God wanted in a king. One thing I've learned in the church is that leadership is servanthood. The world sees leadership as a means of control—the leader is the one who has the most power. You start on the bottom and work your way up. Eventually, if you make it to the top, you have all the people below serving you.

The Bible turns that notion of leadership upside down. "Whoever wants to be the most important must be last of all and servant of all" (Mark 9:35 NCV). A man in the secular world wants to know how many people are serving him, but a man in the kingdom of God wants to know how many people he is serving. A leader meets the needs of others, cares for them, and is their servant. That is the quality God is seeking in His leaders, and it's something you cannot easily see on the outside.

Private Person

In our society, we have a tendency to look for the public person; the man or woman who is good up front. But the Lord is not always looking for a public person, sometimes He seeks out a private person. In fact, many of the leaders God called to change the world have been plucked from very secluded environments. He didn't find Moses leading a political party, but tending sheep in the desert. He didn't find Joseph running a big corporation, but doing time in a prison. He didn't find David leading people in a public marketplace, but out in the hills around Bethlehem, where his only companions were sheep. Nobody could see him, and nobody could know what was in his heart except the Lord who was preparing David to become a great leader.

You see, David wasn't wasting his time tending sheep. He was learning lessons that would prepare him for leading the country. In fact, the single most important event that rocketed David into the public eye was his killing Goliath, and that was based almost entirely on skills he had learned while alone in the fields, watching over his sheep. When King Saul tried to keep him from going out to do battle with the giant, David said, "Thy servant kept his father's sheep, and there came a lion, and a bear, and took a lamb out of the flock: and I went out after him, and smote him, and delivered it out of his mouth: and when he arose against me, I caught him by his beard, and smote him, and slew him. Thy servant slew both the lion and the bear: and this uncircumcised Philistine shall be as one of them" (1 Samuel 17:34–36). Once Saul heard that explanation, he said to David, "Go, and the Lord be with thee" (1 Samuel 17:37).

The private David was forced onto the public stage. All Israel was gathered together, watching David face a giant on the center stage. Yet he had been prepared for this moment by the times he had spent alone in the hills. The daily battles he had fought in protecting his sheep and learning how to be courageous had equipped him to do battle with Goliath. In the quietness of everyday life David was readied for his moment in the spotlight.

That's where God prepares His people. Young people going to college need to know that it is the hours of studying that prepare them for important jobs later in life. Young men heading toward the ministry need to know that it is the personal discipline of their quiet time which readies them for leading people through a public ministry. Being a pastor is not so much about preaching to a congregation on Sunday morning as it is about serving people and spending quiet time alone with God so that you can know what He wants you to say. God is looking for a special spirit in leaders, who will work to obey Him privately so that He can use them publicly. While we want a person who seems "gifted" on the outside, the Lord wants a person who is devoted on the inside.

THE RESPONSE TO ANOINTING IS GOD'S

In 1 Samuel 16, the Lord revealed to Samuel who should be the next king over Israel. So Samuel points at David, says that he is God's choice, and anoints him with oil. We have no way of knowing if David understood what was going on.

David was about sixteen when Samuel poured the oil on his head, and he didn't become king until he was thirty. In the intervening years, he did two things: First, he went back to tending his sheep. Second, he had to keep running away from Saul, who kept trying to kill him. It may not sound exactly like the anointed life, but that's what took place for the next fourteen years. Yet I believe one thing was significantly different in David's life, for when Samuel poured the oil on his head, the Bible records that "the Spirit of the Lord came upon David from that day forward" (1 Samuel 16:13).

When a person is filled with the Spirit of God, everything in life has a new quality. David wasn't the king yet, but he knew he would be one day. God was with David in a special way from that day forward. And the best news is that God is with us in that same way, for we have been given His Spirit. Ephesians tells us that we are to be "filled with the Spirit," and notes that when we are, it smoothes out our relationships with our spouses, our children, and our employers. When we are filled with God's Spirit, Jesus Christ is reflected in our lives. The day Samuel poured oil on David's head, a transition took place. The Bible says that the Spirit of the Lord departed from Saul and resided on David. He was anointed by God with power, becoming the king-in-waiting.

Two thoughts come to mind as we look at the anointing of David. First, God is doing His work at a time when we are not aware of it. The day Samuel was walking through Israel, trying to locate God's new choice as king, David was out in the fields, watching over his sheep. He didn't know God was arranging a great work. He didn't know the Lord had selected him to be the next king of Israel. God was at work even when David wasn't aware of it. The same is true in our own lives. God is working, even though we might not realize it. We need to be faithful and obedient to Him, encouraged by the fact that He has a plan and hasn't forgotten us. He will use us in His own perfect time.

Second, God is doing His work in a way we are not acquainted with. One of the reasons we cannot always see God work is because His ways are often hidden from us. His ways are very different from our ways, so that we cannot recognize His hand. But God continues to work in our lives. When David thought he was just tending his sheep, he was actually being prepared for greatness.

God sought David, found him, commanded him, and anointed him. Though David was just a shepherd boy, he was God's choice to lead Israel. In the same way, God is choosing and preparing His people today. Our job is to be faithful and obedient, and wait to see His plan unfold at the proper time.

APPLICATION

1. Why did the Jews ask Samuel to give them a king?

   a. In what way had they "rejected" God when they asked for a king?

   b. What should they have done instead?

2. In your own words, what is the difference between the way men choose a leader and the way God chooses a leader?

3. Take a look at 1 Samuel 16. When Samuel visited Jesse's house, what kind of man was he looking for?

   a. According to verse 7, what is different about the way the Lord sees people?

b. What does it mean when it says, "the Lord looks at the heart"?

4. In our own day, how do you notice people looking at the "outside" of others?

a. Why is that a mistake?

b. When have you made a mistake about someone's character by looking merely at their "outside"?

5. How is leadership linked to service?

a. Why is a spirit of servanthood necessary to be a godly leader?

b. How do we know David had the spirit of servanthood?

6. In what ways do you see our culture becoming enamored with "public" people?

   a. How do we know that David was a private person?

   b. Why do you suppose God often calls private people into public leadership?

7. How did David's private life prepare him for public leadership?

   a. What private things in your life have prepared you for a greater influence or leadership role?

b. What counsel would you give to a young person who complained, "I spend all my time reading books and taking tests. It seems like I'm going nowhere!"

8. How long was the interval between David's anointing and his coronation?

   a. What did he do during that time?

   b. What encouragement does that bring to your own life?

DID YOU KNOW?

When Jesus Christ is referred to in the New Testament as "the Messiah" (John 1:41), "Messiah" translates the Greek word *christos*, which means "anointed," and from which our English word Christ derives. "Messiah" is a transliteration (put into English letters) of the Hebrew (Old Testament) word for "anointed," *mashiach*. Anointing was primarily used as a way to inaugurate the reign of kings, as well as to identify some prophets and priests. The idea that a great king, a son of David, would be anointed to rule over Israel was a common theme in the Old Testament (Psalm 2:2; 89; 132; Jeremiah 23:5–6; 33:17–22), and was fulfilled at Jesus' baptism when He was anointed by the Holy Spirit (Matthew 3:16–17).

SAUL'S MOODS AND DAVID'S MUSIC

1 Samuel 16:14–23

*In this lesson we will learn, along with a king,
how to serve and soothe the stressed.*

OUTLINE

When God rejected Saul, He allowed an evil spirit to torment the king. That led to the suggestion that a skillful musician come and soothe the king's spirit, opening up the door for David to get the training he needed to be king.

   I.   **The Intruding Spirit**

  II.   **The Interesting Suggestion**

 III.   **The Inspired Selection**

  IV.   **The Insignificant Servant**

   V.   **The Intriguing Solution**

It was the darkest day of my life. Uncertainty flooded my heart and mind. My wife had been taken to the hospital, and no one could tell us what the problem was. She remained there for six days while doctors tested her and tried to discover the problem. They couldn't tell me anything, nor could I tell anyone else what was happening because I didn't know what to say. I'd never been through a more difficult experience. I found myself driving around the streets of the city, listening to the same song on a cassette tape over and over again. "Through It All," by Andrae Crouch, was God's song for me. It ministered to my soul, serving as a reminder that if we never experienced trouble, we would never learn to trust the Lord. I don't know if it was the melody, the words, or the musician, but God used that song to help me when I was facing a tough time.

As I look back over my life, I've found that the Lord often used a song to help me through a particular time. Music is a powerful tool. If our purpose is to glorify God, one of the ways we do that is through the praise and worship of music. It's unfortunate that in some churches music has become a prelude and something else is the focus of worship. Music is a means for moving our spirits toward God. There is a personal ministry to music that touches the discouraged heart, expresses the gladness of a joyous heart, and offers therapy to the soul. It has been said that music has charms to soothe the savage breast, to soften rocks, to bend the knotted oak. Music can cast aside the stresses of life, bringing us encouragement and peace.

Every time you open your Bible, you are opening a wonderful hymnbook. The book of Psalms contains 150 songs that God wanted us to have so that we could explore the joy of music as an expression to Him. The lesson of 1 Samuel 16 is not simply that David was anointed to rule, but that he was also willing to serve.

THE INTRUDING SPIRIT

Something had happened to Saul that changed him. He had failed to obey God's command to totally destroy Amalek, and in doing so he compromised his position as leader. Instead of destroying things, they spared the best. He took God's command and interpreted it in a way that would benefit himself. When the prophet Samuel came and confronted Saul about his disobedience, the king started lying and making up excuses. He even offered to sacrifice some of the lambs to God. But Samuel gave him a great lesson: to obey is better than sacrifice. Because of Saul's disobedience, the Lord rejected him as king. That's when we find this verse: "But the Spirit of the Lord departed from Saul, and an evil spirit from the Lord troubled him" (1 Samuel 16:14).

God's Spirit left Saul, and a troubling spirit came to fill that cavity. If God does not rule us, then Satan does. Everyone is either following God or following the devil. Saul had rejected God, so the Lord took away His Spirit, allowing it to be replaced with an evil spirit.

Some Christians today struggle with that thought, but we must remember that the Spirit in those days did not function as He does today. Acts 2 tells us that on the Day of Pentecost, the Holy Spirit came down and indwelt the believers of Christ. Now every believer is indwelt with the Spirit. We cannot lose Him, for He has become a permanent part of our lives, indwelling us forever. But that was not so in the Old Testament. The Spirit did not come to permanently indwell the people of God. Instead, He selectively and temporarily indwelt them for service. For example, the Spirit was sometimes on Samson. But when he compromised his righteous life by sleeping with Delilah and telling his secret, God took His Spirit away from Samson. In the same way, when David sinned with Bathsheba, he understood that he could lose the empowered blessing of God on his life, for he prayed, "Take not Thy Holy Spirit from me. Restore unto me the joy of Thy salvation" (Psalm 51:11–12).

King Saul had been given a special spiritual empowerment for his job. First Samuel 10:9–10 tells us that God gave Saul "another heart," and that "the Spirit of God came upon him" when he became king. But when he rejected God, the Lord took away His Spirit. In His place came an intruding spirit, an evil spirit that terrorized the king. The word literally means the spirit "overwhelmed" Saul, coming at unexpected times to fill him with terror and discouragement. The poet Robert Browning once wrote a poem about Saul, depicting him in a dark tent, in a cloud of depression, with a spirit of despair all around. Even the people close to Saul recognized something was wrong. His servants said to him, "an evil spirit from God troubleth thee" (1 Samuel 16:15).

THE INTERESTING SUGGESTION

Saul's servants said to him: "Let our lord now command thy servants, which are before thee, to seek out a man, who is a cunning player on a harp: and it shall come to pass, when the evil spirit from God is upon thee, that he shall play with his hand, and thou shalt be well" (1 Samuel 16:16). I find that an interesting suggestion. Their idea was to find a musician to come and soothe the king's soul, and that worked, to a degree. Unfortunately, it wasn't what he needed. It seems to me that somebody close to Saul should have said, "King, since it's an evil spirit bothering you, you ought to repent and make peace with God! You need to deal with the source of the problem and make it go away. Take care of the reason for your dark cloud and you'll be all right." Instead, those servants sounded like the humanistic counselors of our own day, who tell people how to cover up their problems so that it doesn't hurt, but fail to help people deal with the root of their problem: sin.

So the servants suggested a way to help Saul deal with the pain of his depression. They would look for a talented musician to come and play the harp and help to dispel the king's gloom.

THE INSPIRED SELECTION

Eventually they found the perfect person to soothe the king—David. One of those servants had listened to David play, and told the king that David was "cunning in playing, and a mighty valiant man, and a man of war, and prudent in matters, and a comely person; and the Lord is with him" (verse 18). That one verse reveals an awful lot about David.

First, it says he was a skillful musician. He had been called to play for the king, so he would have to be good. There would be no amateurs, searching for the right note when seated before the royal throne. I can't help but think that all who minister in music today are playing for the King. He expects our best. God doesn't ask us to be perfect, but He does expect us to give our all, and to sing from a heart of love and devotion. I fear that too often Christians act as though the performances in church don't have to be as good as those done commercially in the world. That's wrong, for we are singing to the King of kings, and we are to give Him our best. Apparently while David had walked the hillsides alone with his sheep, he had learned to play his instrument quite well. He had also begun writing hymns and songs of praise. He was ready to give a command performance, playing to soothe his king.

Second, that verse tells us David was a mighty man of valor. He probably got his reputation as a young man willing to fight bears and lions by himself. The servant also told Saul that David was a "man of war," which would have impressed king Saul. Historians say that at that time the Philistines were carrying on numerous border attacks and raids, so it is quite possible David had defended himself or his family property against the enemy. He became known as a man you didn't want to mess with, a man who could be trusted in a difficult situation.

Third, he is called "prudent in matters," which literally means he was able to say and do the right thing at the right time. If the musician was going to be in front of the king, particularly when the king was discouraged, it was imperative that the musician be someone who would not embarrass the king or say something foolish. David was prudent in such matters, a shrewd speaker.

Fourth, David is described as handsome. He was a sharp man, with a natural magnetism. The king would like him, because everybody liked him. That's why women sang of him, and tough soldiers were willing to follow him into the battle. You couldn't be in David's presence without appreciating his qualities.

Fifth, it was simply said of David that "the Lord is with him." It was obvious to those around David that he was a godly man. He lived to please the Lord, and it was evident to everyone. He had a spiritual quality that recommended him to others. And it is simply true that the best musicians in the church are those who are both skillful and godly.

It is important for the growing world of Christian entertainment to keep that in mind. As Christian music cranks out million-selling superstars, we sometimes are blinded by celebrity. If we forget the importance of a godly character in our musicians, replacing it with the mere ability to entertain, the music loses its power. We have at times had professional musicians take over the leadership of a service and offer nothing more than entertainment and their own selfish desire to perform. That's why I'm always impressed with godly performers who simply ask, "What do you need? We want to be a part of what you're doing; tell us what you want and allow us to be a part of your ministry." When that happens, the body of Christ is ministered to. Without it, there is no "Spirit," no depth, and no power to the music.

THE INSIGNIFICANT SERVANT

"Wherefore Saul sent messengers unto Jesse, and said, 'Send me David thy son, which is with the sheep.' And Jesse took an ass laden with bread, and a bottle of wine, and a kid, and sent them by David his son unto Saul" (1 Samuel 16:19–20). Think about the scene for a moment: Here we find the young man who has already been anointed king, on his way to see the failed king, so that he can offer some bread and serenade him with songs. David, the anointed king, walks down that dusty road, lyre slung over his shoulder, leading a donkey on a journey to minister to King Saul. Remember, the Lord had already rejected Saul, and had already made David king. But David was willing to demonstrate his love and faithfulness, strumming his instrument and doing the menial tasks, rather than immediately insisting upon the throne. He was willing to be an insignificant servant, rather than demanding a significant role. What a great example David's life is to all those who desire to be used in significant ways by the Lord!

THE INTRIGUING SOLUTION

The next few verses are remarkable:

And David came to Saul, and stood before him: and he loved him greatly, and he became his armorbearer. And Saul sent to Jesse, saying, "Let David, I pray thee, stand before me; for he hath found favor in my sight." And it came to pass, when the spirit from God was upon Saul, that David took a harp and played with his hand: so Saul was refreshed, and was well, and the evil spirit departed from him (1 Samuel 16:21–23).

The words translated "stood before him" mean that David reported for duty to his king. David must have had a tremendous attitude if he was willing to be the servant to the man he knew he would replace. The greatest way to express love is through service. When we serve one another, we build a bond of love. That's why Jesus washed the disciples' feet, to help them see the importance of stooping to meet each other's needs.

We see evident in David's life the principle that love grows out of ministry. When Saul would get depressed, David would start to sing, and it always refreshed the king. As we minister to others, love grows in our hearts.

A second principle we see is that ministry is like soothing music to a depressed man. Ministry helps heal and comfort, the same way music does.

One last principle I find in David's life is that serving is good training for leading. There was no better place David could go to learn how to be a king. God found a way to get him some training, so that when the time came to take the throne, David would be prepared. He watched what went on, learned the protocol of the palace, and was ready to move right into his proper place as king over Israel when Saul died.

But none of that training would have happened if David had been unwilling to serve. If you want to be a leader, you must first learn how to be a server. God can use your gifts to serve, and in that way train you for the next step.

APPLICATION

1. What kind of music do you like best?

   a. What kind of music do you not like?

   b. How can music soothe or annoy us?

2. What has been the most difficult time in your life?

   a. What helped get you through it?

   b. When have you found that music has been able to comfort and soothe your spirit?

3. Why did God allow an evil spirit to torment the king?

   a. As you look at King Saul's predicament, what do you think of the servants' advice?

   b. What advice would you have offered?

   c. If a friend of yours, who you knew had walked away from God, told you he was seeing a counselor to help him deal with his guilt, what would you tell him?

d. Why do suggestions that deal with *symptoms* but not with *causes* bring more harm than good?

4. Have you ever found yourself depressed and discouraged because of your own disobedience to God? When? What were the circumstances?

   a. What helped pull you out of it?

   b. What would you say to someone who told you, "My life has been a mess ever since I stopped walking with God"?

5. Can a Christian "lose" the Holy Spirit? Why or why not?

   a. What does John 10:27–29 have to say about that?

   b. How is the work of the Spirit different in our own day than in David's day?

6. Take a look at the way David is described in 1 Samuel 16:18. What words do you think people would use to describe you?

   a. What qualities would you most like to develop?

7. How do you see Christians embracing celebrity?

   a. How can that be dangerous?

   b. What qualities do you think are most important in the lives of those Christians who live in the public eye?

8. If you were David, would you have struggled with the call to be Saul's servant? Why?

   a. How can love grow out of ministry?

   b. When have you found that occurring in your own life?

   c. In what way is ministry like soothing music to those in misery?

DID YOU KNOW?

One of the clearest differences between the Old Testament and the New Testament is the role of the Holy Spirit. In the Old Testament, the Holy Spirit is said to be "in the midst" of Israel on different occasions (Isaiah 63:11; Haggai 2:5). In addition to a national presence, the Spirit came upon certain individuals to equip them for service: craftsmen (Exodus 31:3), judges (Judges 3:10; 6:34), and kings (1 Samuel 16:13). Generally, the Holy Spirit had a temporary presence in the Old Testament. The New Testament role of the Spirit can be summed up from Romans 8:9—the Holy Spirit indwells every child of God fully and permanently.

WHEN TWO GIANTS MEET

1 Samuel 17:1–38

In this lesson we will learn how to trust God for victory in our lives.

OUTLINE

The story of David and Goliath is not simply a children's tale. It is a story of the eternal struggle between good and evil. From it we can see the results that come as we put our trust in God.

I. **The Challenge to the Living God**
   A. The Scene of the Challenge
   B. The Size of the Challenge
   C. The Shout of the Challenge
   D. The Seriousness of the Challenge

II. **The Champion of the Living God**
   A. He Was Consistent in the Routine Things
   B. He Was Challenged by the Impossible Things
   C. He Was Committed in Spite of Ridicule
   D. He Was Courageous in the Lord
   E. He Was Confident in the Spirit

III. **The Conquest by the Living God**
   A. The Instruments of David
   B. The Insult to God
   C. The Intimidation of the Giant
   D. The Impact of a Champion

Have you ever faced giants? I don't mean literal giants, of course, but problems of such huge magnitude they loomed as giants on the horizon? As a believer, you need to be reminded that God is with you, even when facing giants. The God who helped David defeat the giant of his day is the same God who lives and supports us today. And the principles of victory that are found in David's story are transferable concepts to our lives today.

THE CHALLENGE TO THE LIVING GOD

First Samuel 17 is not just a story about a young man fighting a grown giant. It is a story about the conflict of the ages. It is a story about the battle that has been raging since Satan first rebelled against God. The confrontation is between good and evil, between God and Satan. It is the story of a challenge to the living God by the devil and his forces of evil, and it all takes place in a moment's time, in the Valley of Elah.

The Scene of the Challenge

Picture the scene:

> Now the Philistines gathered their armies together to battle, and were gathered together at Shochoh, which belongs to Judah; they encamped between Shochoh and Azekah, in Ephes-dammim. And Saul and the men of Israel were gathered together, and they encamped in the valley of Elah, and drew up in battle array against the Philistines. The Philistines stood on a mountain on one side, and Israel stood on a mountain on the other side, with a valley between them (1 Samuel 17:1–3 NKJV).

The setting is not hard to imagine. In fact, there is a place in Israel today purported to be the very site where the battle took place, a deep ravine between two giant cliffs. The army of the Philistines was gathered on one side, the army of Israel on the other. Down in the valley between the two cliffs is the place where the challenge was issued, and where the battle would be fought. The gap between the two cliffs is only one hundred yards wide, and that's the place where God's representative and Satan's representative will meet.

The Size of the Challenge

And a champion went out from the camp of the Philistines,
named Goliath, from Gath, whose height was six cubits
and a span. He had a bronze helmet on his head, and he
was armed with a coat of mail, and the weight of the coat was
five thousand shekels of bronze. And he had bronze armor
on his legs and a bronze javelin between his shoulders.
Now the staff of his spear was like a weaver's beam, and
his iron spearhead weighed six hundred shekels; and a
shield-bearer went before him" (1 Samuel 17:4–7 NKJV).

The size of the challenge is clear: it is the size of Goliath. He
was from Gath, a place where the spies sent by Moses to check out
the Promised Land had reported seeing giants. They referred to the
giants as "the sons of Anak," and many years later Joshua would
destroy many of the Anakim cities. In fact, Joshua would leave only
three cities standing—including Gath, from where Goliath came.
He stood "six cubits and a span," which means he was somewhere
between 9'6" and 9'9". That would make him at least two feet taller
than the biggest players in professional basketball. And he wasn't
tall and skinny, like some tall basketball players. Goliath was
strong and wide, a huge man who probably weighed four or five
hundred pounds.

Not only that, he was armed with a brass helmet, brass leggings,
a coat of chain mail that weighed about 250 pounds, and a spear
with a shaft like a telephone pole. Just the point of the spear
weighted between 15 and 20 pounds! In front of Goliath came a
shield bearer, who tried to keep any stray arrows from hitting the
giant. David was facing a mammoth challenge.

The Shout of the Challenge

Then he stood and cried out to the armies of Israel, and said
to them, "Why have you come out to line up for battle?
Am I not a Philistine, and you the servants of Saul? Choose
a man for yourselves, and let him come down to me. If he
is able to fight with me and kill me, then we will be your
servants: but if I prevail against him and kill him, then you
shall be our servants and serve us." And the Philistine said,
"I defy the armies of Israel this day; give me a man, that we
may fight together" (1 Samuel 17:8–10 NKJV).

This was one of the few times in history that two nations decided
to settle their battles representatively. Rather than wipe out the

other side, and lose all those potential servants, the Philistines wanted to settle the fight economically. One man would represent one side, another man would represent the other side. They'd fight it out, and whoever wins, that nation gets the victory. Goliath shouted for Israel to send someone to fight him, but nobody on Israel's side wanted to take him up on the challenge.

The Seriousness of the Challenge

"And the Philistine drew near morning and evening, and presented himself forty days," (1 Samuel 17:16). Goliath didn't offer a one-time threat. He came every day for six weeks, standing in the valley and shouting out his threats. Every morning and evening the Israelites had to listen to his taunts, but no one volunteered. In fact, the giant's challenge began to disturb the soldiers of Israel, and verse 11 tells us they became "dismayed and greatly afraid." Here was a pagan, causing the army of God to stand powerless in fear.

We can all feel that way at times. The battles we face can feel insurmountable—beyond our capacity to stand up and fight. And for me, they always feel worse in the morning when I first get up and think about them, and at night when my head hits the pillow. That is exactly the situation that faced the Israelites. They were confronted with a challenge for which they had no answer.

THE CHAMPION OF THE LIVING GOD

It would take a champion to face that sort of challenge, and David had the heart of a champion. If someone has the heart of a champion, age doesn't matter. Champions today are made of the same stuff as David. One of the things I've noticed in life is that there are certain characteristics to champions. When we talk about champions for the Lord, we invariably talk about the same attributes we see in the life of David.

He Was Consistent in the Routine Things

Now David was the son of that Ephrathite of Bethlehem-judah, whose name was Jesse; and he had eight sons: and the man went among men for an old man in the days of Saul. And the three eldest sons of Jesse went and followed Saul to the battle: and the names of his three sons that went to the battle were Eliab the firstborn, and next unto him Abinadab, and the third Shammah. And David was the youngest: and the three eldest followed Saul. But David went and returned from Saul to feed his father's sheep at Bethlehem (1 Samuel 17:12–15).

David's father told him to take some food to the three boys at war. I find it interesting that while his three older brothers went to war, David was sent back to his sheep. He had been called to play for King Saul at times, but now that Saul was busy with war plans, David was back in the fields. Again, even though he had been anointed and was waiting to take over the kingship of Israel, he was comfortable serving as shepherd for his father and part-time guitarist for Saul. David refused to violate the routine, or to jump ahead of God's schedule. When asked to be an errand boy, taking sandwiches to his brothers at the battlefront, David obeyed. I admire his willingness to do the menial tasks and to take care of the small things.

There is an interesting insight into David's heart in verse 20: "And David rose up early in the morning, and left the sheep with a keeper, and took, and went, as Jesse had commanded him; and he came to the trench, as the host was going forth to the fight and shouted for the battle." David was faithful to take care of his responsibilities, even in the little details. It must have been thrilling for a boy to run off and see the armies, but he didn't use the opportunity of something exciting to neglect the routine things of his life. He made sure somebody was caring for his sheep before leaving. That sort of consistency is always true of great champions. It may even be the difference between the champions and the runners-up. Champions are willing to concentrate on the details that go unnoticed by others. They are willing to follow the routine, even when nobody else is watching. There is no shortage of people with the desire to win, but there is often a shortage of people with the desire to prepare to win. David wasn't afraid to prepare. He did the routine things carefully.

He Was Challenged by the Impossible Things

And as he talked with them, behold, there came up the champion, the Philistine of Gath, Goliath by name, out of the armies of the Philistines, and spake according to the same words: and David heard them. And all the men of Israel, when they saw the man, fled from him, and were sore afraid (1 Samuel 17:23–24).

As soon as David got to the soldier's camp, he rushed to see his brothers and take them their food. As they stood talking, Goliath made his daily trek to the valley in order to shout his challenge to God's people. But after David heard it, he looked around and saw his fellow Jews running away. So he began asking questions, found out who Goliath was, and was also told that King Saul had promised great riches to the soldier willing to take on the giant. Not only that, the winner could marry Saul's daughter. Of course, the only reason Saul had created this particular incentive was because he was a coward. Saul stood head and shoulders above all the other Israelites, and he was their king, so he should have been the one out fighting the giant. But Saul was afraid, operating in the flesh, and refusing to trust God. So David decided to volunteer.

He Was Committed in Spite of Ridicule

I never yet met a champion who didn't look at the impossible and say, "We can do that." But champions are often targets. When a man decides to be a champion for God, he sets himself up for a lot of criticism. If a woman decides she wants to be more than average, and do something magnificent for God, she can be certain she'll be attacked by somebody. And David, in volunteering to fight the giant, was confronted by his own brother:

> And Eliab his eldest brother heard when he spake unto the men; and Eliab's anger was kindled against David, and he said, "Why camest thou down hither? And with whom have you left those few sheep in the wilderness? I know thy pride, and the naughtiness of thine heart; for thou art come down that thou mightest see the battle" (verse 28).

Eliab was a man of great stature, and doubtless he had some ability. Perhaps, when Samuel had visited their home, he had thought, "Hey, I can be king." But God wasn't choosing based on outward appearances, and David had a heart for God that Eliab didn't have. It must have rankled the older brother, and now young David was asking questions about this giant that Eliab was afraid of, so he begins criticizing his brother. Right away David is faced with a challenge: he can fight the critic, or fight the giant. Every champion has to make a decision like that sooner or later. Anybody who sets out to do something great will face ridicule, and they can choose to battle the critic or stay focused on the task. David chose not to fight with his brother, instead saying, "What have I done?" (1 Samuel 17:29). I'm not the enemy—Goliath is. Let's stay on task.

But Eliab wasn't the only hurdle David faced. He next goes to see King Saul, who tells him, "Thou art not able to go against this Philistine to fight with him: for thou art but a youth, and he a man of war from his youth" (verse 33). In other words, "You're just a kid. You're overmatched. You can't do it." When you want to do something great, there will always be somebody around to tell you that you can't do it. It's usually someone who doesn't have the courage to do it themselves. Saul was afraid, so he told David it was impossible. But David knew who he was fighting, so he didn't get into a battle with Eliab, or argue with Saul. He just kept his eyes on the goal.

He Was Courageous in the Lord

And David said unto Saul, "Thy servant kept his father's sheep, and there came a lion, and a bear, and took a lamb out of the flock: And I went out after him, and smote him, and delivered it out of his mouth: and when he arose against me, I caught him by his beard, and smote him, and slew him. Thy servant slew both the lion and the bear; and this uncircumcised Philistine shall be as one of them, seeing he hath defied the armies of the living God." David said moreover, "The Lord that delivered me out of the paw of the lion, and out of the paw of the bear, He will deliver me out of the hand of this Philistine." And Saul said unto David, "Go, and the LORD be with thee" (1 Samuel 17:34–37).

David isn't being a braggart. He doesn't exclaim, "I can do it!" Instead, he notes that God has been on his side in the past, so he can trust that God will be on his side in the future. He finds courage in the Lord. His past victories encouraged his present success. He said the same thing when facing the giant, explaining, "Thou comest to me with a sword, and with a spear, and with a shield: but I come to thee in the name of the Lord of hosts, the God of the armies of Israel, whom thou hast defied" (verse 45). David recognized his power was in God—the same place we find our courage today. In Christ we can do all things, without Him, we can do nothing.

He Was Confident in the Spirit

When David volunteered, Saul tried to talk him out of it. When he couldn't be dissuaded, Saul tried to put his armor on David. But since Saul was so big, the Scripture says that David couldn't even walk once he had it on! The helmet must have rattled around on his head, and the breastplate would have weighed him down, so that once David had all this protective gear on, he couldn't even move. Instead of relying on that sort of protection, David basically said, "Thanks, but no thanks," and took it all off. You see, David wasn't going to fight Goliath in the outward man. He was going to fight with the inward man. Even with his armor, Saul had been afraid to fight, so it wasn't the armor which was going to make a difference. David was going to go out and meet the giant in the confidence of the Spirit, armed with all he needed to fight the giant.

THE CONQUEST BY THE LIVING GOD

The end of the story is truly exciting, for God reveals that He is more powerful than any man, or any manmade weapon. The end of the story reveals the triumph of good; the conquest by the living God.

The Instruments of David

All David chose to take with him were a staff, a sling, and five smooth stones which he put into his shepherd's bag. Rather than relying on armor and shields, David was relying on God.

The Insult to God

Imagine what Goliath must have thought. He had been coming into that valley every day for six weeks, waiting for somebody brave enough to meet him in battle, and all he saw were terrified soldiers. Then this day he sees a boy, with no armor or weapons, no shield or armor bearer. He must have scratched his eyes at the sight. Verse 42 says that Goliath "disdained" David, which literally means he curled his lip. "Am I a dog, that thou comest to me with staves?" Goliath asked, cursing David by his gods. "Come to me, and I will give thy flesh unto the fowls of the air, and to the beasts of the field" (verses 43–44). Goliath probably used the name of Dagon, whom David knew to be a false god. It was an insult to the Lord.

The Intimidation of the Giant

Then said David to the Philistine, "Thou comest to me with a sword, and with a spear, and with a shield: but I come to thee in the name of the Lord of hosts, the God of the armies of Israel, whom thou hast defied. This day the Lord will deliver thee into mine hand; and I will smite thee and take thine head from thee; and I will give the carcasses of the host of the Philistines this day unto the fowls of the air, and to the wild beasts of the earth; that all the earth may know that there is a God in Israel. And all this assembly shall know that the Lord saveth not with sword and spear: for the battle is the Lord's, and He will give you into our hands" (1 Samuel 17:45–47).

As I read those words, I realize that this was the moment of truth. David has just infuriated the biggest bully on the block, and if God isn't on David's side, he's going to die. Not only that, but the

Lord had made a promise to redeem mankind through David's line, so if David dies, the promised redemption is over. David purposely intimidated Goliath, and in doing so set himself up to win the battle.

The Impact of a Champion

Goliath got so angry at David's words that he rushed forward, not even bothering to put on his helmet. But David raced also, taking out a stone and hurling it into the forehead of that giant. The Bible says that he fell face down, and that big guy in his armor must have made quite a noise going down. Then David ran up, struggled to pull out the giant's sword, and chopped Goliath's head off. The scene on both sides of that valley must have been something special. Neither side could believe it. The Israelites must have thought, "Did I just see what I think I saw?" And the Philistines must have been saying, "Uh-oh. We're in trouble now."

Think about the lessons of this story. God won that victory with a teenager, a sling, a stone, and a borrowed sword. He loves to use foolish things in order to confound the wise. God conquered that giant, and in that is a wonderful lesson. We all face giants every day. We have the challenge of trying to live as Christians in a lost world, and like David we need to be willing to confront our problems. Saul wouldn't do that—he stood around for forty days, trying to pass his problem off to somebody else. Saul was a coward, refusing to walk with God. David was courageous, making sure to rely on the Lord. Confront your problems in the courage of the Lord.

There's one other thing we learn from this story, and that is the importance of cherishing our trophies. I don't mean we need to live in the past, but that we shouldn't bury our victories. It's the trophies that reveal we are winners, and they encourage us to keep facing challenges. Verse 54 says that David took Goliath's armor and put it in his tent, as a memorial to the great work God had done.

Finally, as you face the tough things in life, concentrate on your goals. David's goal was to vindicate the living God. He didn't care what Eliab thought, or how Saul reacted, he only cared about God. When we choose to follow Him faithfully, we can be sure God will be with us as we focus on achieving great things for Him.

APPLICATION

1. How would you describe the emotions of the Israelite soldiers as they sat and listened to Goliath's daily challenge?

   a. Have you felt like that when facing a daunting task?

   b. What did you do about it?

2. In your view, what makes a champion?

   a. Why is consistency in routine things important?

   b. What routine things did David continue doing?

3. What problems do you need to confront?

   a. What future goals do you have that you feel you should start working toward?

DID YOU KNOW?

David was not the only Israelite who was handy with a sling. Judges 20:15–16 tells of 700 select Benjamite warriors, all of whom were left-handed, who could sling a stone at a target as thin as a hair—and hit it every time. Slingstones were smooth, one-pound stones which traveled at speeds of 90–100 miles per hour. The word in Judges 20:16, describing how the Benjamites would not "miss," is the Hebrew verb *chata*, which means "to miss, go wrong, sin." The military use of the term "to miss" a target became a useful word for describing what it meant to miss a moral target, or to sin against God's law. Our modern definition of sin—to miss God's mark—is perfectly illustrated by missing the mark with a slingstone. Just as missing the target with a sling in battle could have disastrous consequences, so can missing God's target in our lives.

THE HIGH COST OF SUCCESS

1 Samuel 17:55–18:16

In this lesson we will learn how to handle some of life's greatest challenges.

OUTLINE

When David killed Goliath, his entire life changed. His success brought him tremendous pressure, and created a whole new life for him. In this chapter we will explore the changes in David's life, and the way he coped with them.

   I.   **David's Success Created a New Family**

   II. **David's Success Created a New Fame**

   III. **David's Success Created a New Foe**

   IV. **David's Success Created a New Friend**

   V.   **David's Keys for Surviving Success**

What do the following names have in common: Vince Lombardi, Red Auerbach, Casey Stengle, and John Wooden? Sure, they're all famous coaches, and they are all in the Hall of Fame for their respective sports. But that's not all. They have all won back-to-back championships. It's very difficult to become a champion once, but it's almost impossible to do it twice in a row. Look through the list of winners in any sport, and you'll find only a handful of teams who won the championship two years running. But Stengle did it in baseball with the Yankees. Vince Lombardi did it twice in football with the Green Bay Packers. Wooden won six straight titles in basketball at UCLA. And Red Auerbach's Boston Celtics won the NBA championship almost every year for more than a decade.

There is something about being successful, about climbing the mountain to its peak, that affects people so that they are unable to repeat it. Often the team is young, the players are the same, and the coaching staff has remained intact, but they still can't get it done. It's tough to win, but even tougher to repeat. I think of that when I read about David's life after killing Goliath. On that day, David opened up a whole new chapter to his life. He would never again be the lowly shepherd boy. The pressures that come with success found their way into David's life. There is a descriptive phrase in 1 Samuel 18 that appears three times, and it is the phrase, "he behaved wisely." In verse 5 we read, "David went out whithersoever Saul sent him, and behaved himself wisely." In verse 14 we find, "David behaved himself wisely in all his ways." And in verse 30 we see these words; "and it came to pass, after they went forth, that David behaved himself more wisely than all the servants of Saul; so that his name was much set by." To behave oneself wisely is commensurate with being successful.

David's success began when he killed the giant. It continued in everything else he did. The young shepherd boy had come a long way, and he followed up his success with wise behavior. You know, few people can survive success. For every hundred people who survive adversity, there is only one who survives prosperity. But David had to pay the high cost of success.

DAVID'S SUCCESS CREATED A NEW FAMILY

As David made his way down into the valley to fight Goliath, King Saul had turned to the commander of the army and asked,

"Whose son is this youth?" (1 Samuel 17:55). Some people have tried to say that this verse shows an error in the Bible, since David had already been playing the harp to soothe Saul's moods. But Saul does not ask who David is; he asks who David's father is. David was not unknown to the king, but his father was. In order to fulfill his promises to the victor over Goliath, Saul needed to identify David's father. Jesse was about to be made tax free in Israel and taken off the tax rolls; and he needed to be notified that David would not be returning home to live.

With David's success came the creation of a new family. He had been conscripted into the king's service, and was now to live with the royal family and to marry Saul's daughter. Overnight David had his life turned upside down. The silence of the hillside was to be replaced by the noise of the palace. The solitude of the sheep was to be pushed aside for the multitude of admirers who thronged David wherever he went. Success often brings overwhelming changes. Life is never the same after a huge success. We sometimes covet success, not knowing the radical changes it involves. David was taken from his own family to be with and marry into the king's family.

DAVID'S SUCCESS CREATED A NEW FAME

The NIV translates 1 Samuel 18:5–7 this way:

> Whatever Saul sent him to do, David did it so successfully that Saul gave him a high rank in the army. This pleased all the people, and Saul's officers as well. When the men were returning home after David had killed the Philistine, the women came out from all the towns of Israel to meet King Saul with singing and dancing, with joyful songs and with tambourines and lutes. As they danced, they sang: "Saul has slain his thousands, and David his tens of thousands."

David had a newfound fame. Suddenly everybody was singing about his triumph. He was a national hero, though a week earlier nobody had ever heard of him. Even his own brothers had disdained him. Now everyone is singing his name. The people loved him. Even Saul's officers liked him. He was an overnight success, and that meant he had to live with the pain of recognition.

It's funny how a little recognition can ruin a person. I once read of a famous preacher who had warned seminary students that popularity is a dangerous state, because it easily leads to pride and compromise. Watch out for desiring popularity, for if not kept in perspective, it can have a deadly effect. Success is like a drug: the more you have, the more you want. That's why it would have been easy for David to let his popularity go to his head. Instead, he acted wisely by remaining close to the Lord.

DAVID'S SUCCESS CREATED A NEW FOE

Unfortunately, David's success got him a new enemy. When Saul heard the people singing about David's triumph, he became jealous. They were acclaiming David's courage, as well they should, but in doing so Saul thought they were criticizing his lack of leadership. Even though God had already told Saul that his kingdom would be taken away, he became envious of David, seeing him as a threat. The king must have been looking over his shoulder, wondering when God might give the kingdom to David, for the words to that song asked, "What more can he have but the kingdom?" David already had the praise of the people. He was already adored by the women. He was popular with everyone, even the military leadership. The only thing left was to be crowned king.

Jealousy took over Saul's heart. It would eat at him, at times even tempting him to murder. The Bible says that on two different occasions Saul was in such a bad mood that he threw a spear at David, trying to pin him to the wall. Saul became suspicious, jealous, afraid, and filled with fear. Verse 29 even notes that "Saul became David's enemy continually."

Now this situation would probably cause jealousy even if the man at the center of it was better balanced than Saul. Remember, Saul was sick, tormented by an evil spirit. His kingship was not yet a well-established institution in Israel. To maintain his position, Saul had to be recognized as the strongest man in the kingdom. His authority rested almost entirely on his military achievements, and suddenly his glory had been eclipsed by another. Three times in this chapter we're told that David's success prompted fear in the king. Verse 12 says: "And Saul was afraid of David, because the Lord was with him, and was departed from Saul." He became apprehensive, watching David out of the corner of his eye, knowing there was something special about the boy. Verse 15 again says the king was afraid, though that word can also be translated "in awe" of David. Saul was impressed that everything the young man touched turned out right. And verses 28–29 reveal that Saul was afraid of David because even the king's own daughter was in love with him. The people closest to Saul were choosing David over the king.

It was obvious to everyone that the Lord was present in David's life. And when God is evident in your life, you are bound to make enemies, especially of those who are not living right. John the Baptist lived a holy life, and it caused Herod to live in fear of him. Jesus Christ lived a holy life, and it caused people to hate Him. Men who have experienced great success have noted that it is difficult to maintain friendships with people they knew before their success—jealousy creates troubles. Friendships come hard, but enemies come easy. David's success created a new foe, and the rest of Saul's life he would create troubles for David.

DAVID'S SUCCESS CREATED A NEW FRIEND

We come now to one of the most special aspects of David's story:

> And it came to pass, when he had made an end of speaking unto Saul, that the soul of Jonathan was knit with the soul of David, and Jonathan loved him as his own soul. And Saul took him that day, and would let him go no more home to his father's house. Then Jonathan and David made a covenant, because he loved him as his own soul. And Jonathan stripped himself of the robe that was upon him, and gave it to David, and his garments, even to his sword, and to his bow, and to his girdle (1 Samuel 18:1–4).

A true friend is a valuable possession. Sometimes we measure our friends by their affinity to us when we face trouble. Adversity is the litmus test for our fair-weather friends. But at the same time, when you achieve some great success, you also find out who your friends are. I've had successful men tell me they never knew if others were their friends because of who they were or what they could offer. We all want our friends to like us simply because of who we are, not because we can do something for them. David was at a time when he needed a friend he could count on. In the midst of his success, he found Jonathan.

Jonathan had lived through his father's failure to defeat the Philistines. It must have been hard for the boy, watching his father become filled with fear and unwilling to confront the enemy of God. The Spirit of the Lord had departed from Saul, and all that was left was the shell of a man. Jonathan must have watched in anguish as his father refused to act, then concocted some incentive plan to find somebody who would fight Goliath.

But when David came marching back with Goliath's armor, Jonathan must have felt relief that the conflict was over, glad that the pressure on his father was off, and excitement that God had worked so wonderfully through another young man. Jonathan saw what David did, recognized his courage, and loved David as himself. The two became fast friends. Jonathan stood by David as he hid from King Saul. Jonathan served as a go-between, pleading with his father for David's life. Somehow he and David were able to maintain a relationship, even though it meant choosing between a friend and a father.

If you go through the pressures of success, it's nice to know you have one friend who will stick with you. It's comforting to know you have one person who is not afraid of you, who will stand by you when others walk away, and will say the things you may not want to hear. A friend knows the difference between what you say in a moment of stress and what you really mean in your heart. He can warn you when your defeats are too important to you, or you make too big a thing of your victories. It was good of God to provide that sort of intimate friend for David. And it was good of David to not shield himself from others, thinking there was no one to trust.

DAVID'S KEYS FOR SURVIVING SUCCESS

Success can do some people in. David was able to survive and thrive on success for two basic reasons. First, he refused to be changed by his success. David revealed the same submissive spirit as he'd had before his great victory. That's why the Bible tells us that David did "whatever Saul told him to do." Rather than claiming he was too big for such a task, or insisting on only being given the choice assignments, David did everything he was asked. For example, verse 10 reveals that David continued playing his guitar for the king. Many people would have thought themselves too important for such a menial task, but not David. I've found that many people who find success cease being submissive. A person who used to be perfectly normal now acts completely different. But David wasn't changed. He didn't allow his circumstances to affect his character.

Second, he refused to take credit for his success. David was the least impressed of anybody about his victory over Goliath. He simply reflected the praise toward God, recognizing that it was the Lord who had granted the victory. Instead of reading his press clippings, David praised the Lord. That's really why Saul was so afraid of David. He recognized that David understood the power of God. David started out humble, and in giving praise to God, he remained humble.

APPLICATION

1. Have you ever known anyone who changed because of experiencing big success? Who? What were the circumstances?

   a. How was your friendship impacted by their success?

   b. What advice would you give someone who was starting to experience a big success?

2. What dangers were inherent for David in joining a new family?

   a. What danger is there in fame?

3. Why was Saul afraid of David?

   a. What made Saul hate David?

   b. Would you agree with someone who claimed, "It's easy to spot a Christian—just look at how he lives his life"?

4. When have you experienced opposition because of your walk with God?

a. How did you respond?

b. As believers, why should we expect opposition?

5. What do you think drew David and Jonathan together?

a. What does their friendship say about Jonathan's character and maturity?

6. Why do you think David was so successful?

a. What lessons from his experience can you glean for your own life?

DID YOU KNOW?

The most momentous decision Jonathan, the son of Saul, ever made was to enter into a covenant with David, who had been anointed king of Israel to succeed Saul. This was not just a casual friendship; it was a life-or-death, permanent bonding together of the destinies of David and Jonathan (1 Samuel 18:1–4). Jonathan's decision reflects the truths of Proverbs 18:24b and Luke 14:26—covenant agreements supercede family loyalty. Jonathan remained true to David, and in return, after Jonathan's death, David sought out Mephibosheth, Jonathan's crippled son, and gave him a place at the king's table (2 Samuel 9). Covenant partners will do anything for one another (cf. 1 Samuel 20:4 with John 15:7).

THE FUGITIVE

1 Samuel 18:17–19:24

*In this lesson we will learn how to let go and
let God do all things through us.*

OUTLINE

Not long after David's triumph came David's testing. In running
away from King Saul, David forgot some of the lessons about
trusting God. This lesson will explore the importance of trusting
God regardless of circumstances.

  I. **When You Know God's Promises, You Don't Have to
     Prove Anything**

 II. **When You Know God's Faithfulness, You Don't Have to
     Fear Anything**

III. **When You Know God's Fellowship, You Can Handle Losing
     a Friend**

A few years ago, Dave Hunt wrote two books that rocked the Christian church. In *The Seduction of Christianity* and *Beyond Seduction*, he showed how the growing emphasis on achievement has become a danger to the faith. If a person is an aggressive, success-driven individual, it is hard to deny there is a battle between what the Bible says about depending totally on God, and what our society's current philosophies say about doing it yourself. Mr. Hunt warned of the danger inherent in fantasizing success, and it caused many Christians to stop and ask, "What are our goals, and how do they fit with the things of God?"

Most men of God recorded in Scripture faced those same struggles. There is a war going on between the ego and the Holy Spirit, between doing all we can and letting God do all through us. I don't know a Christian attempting to do great things who hasn't fought the battle between self-control and Spirit-control, so it should come as no surprise that David fought that same battle.

WHEN YOU KNOW GOD'S PROMISES, YOU DON'T HAVE TO PROVE ANYTHING

Fresh from his victory over Goliath and his strong stand for God, David was put into a pressure-filled situation so that God could purge from him dependence on everything but the Lord. That's one of the reasons He still allows us to go through hard times today. It is God's way of dealing with the aggressive and determined. The Lord allows tough times to come in order to keep us centered on Himself alone.

David had first come to King Saul in order to soothe his troubled spirit, and the Bible records that he was effective. We're even told that Saul loved David greatly (1 Samuel 16:21), and made him his armor-bearer. Then, when David killed Goliath, Saul brought the boy into his house, making him almost a member of the family. Whatever the king commanded, David obeyed, and soon all the people loved and appreciated David. Even Saul's own family drew close to David.

But then one day the king overheard women singing David's praises, and he became jealous. He began noticing David's wisdom and walk with the Lord, and it made him afraid. Eventually Saul came to see David as an enemy, even throwing a spear at the boy in an attempt to kill him. The king had promised David his daughter's hand in marriage, but then he cooked up a plan to have David killed. Saul told David that he could marry Saul's daughter Merab if only he would fight in some bloody battles, but David refuses, saying, "Who am I, and what is my life or my father's family in Israel, that I should be son-in-law to the king?" (1 Samuel 18:18). So Merab was married to another man.

Later Saul found out his other daughter, Michal, was in love with David, and he again tried to arrange for David's death. The king invited David to marry Michal. At first David balked, saying that he was too poor and lightly esteemed to be married into the king's family. But Saul insists he is not too poor, and that he will promise his daughter's hand in marriage if David will kill 100 Philistine soldiers. The king thought this would be impossible, and that David would be killed in the process. Instead, David shows up with evidence from 200 Philistine soldiers as a dowry for his new bride. The epitome of the determined, aggressive man, David proved he was worthy of Michal's hand in marriage.

I'm not sure David had the right attitude in this situation. Why was he intent on proving his worth to King Saul? He had already been anointed by God as the next king, why would he grovel? Every time I read this I want to shout, "You're already the king, David! For goodness sake, what's wrong?" But then I think about how we all have a tendency to put ourselves down. I sometimes think half of the things that occur in churches today are to prove we're somehow worthy to God. People want to make themselves more worthwhile, in order to feel better about themselves. But the fact is we do not live and work for acceptance; we live and work *from* acceptance. I don't serve God in order to prove my worth to Him; I serve God because *He has already declared me worthy.* My accomplishments don't add a thing to my value. I am a worthy person in Jesus Christ, who died on the cross to save me from my sins. I don't have to prove anything, or make myself more acceptable, because God has already chosen me and made me acceptable. I am to live in light of what's already happened, not try to make myself good enough for God to accept me.

Our culture has gone crazy over self-esteem, as a way to make up for the fact that people feel guilty because of their sin. But Christians have to remember we do not earn our self-esteem, we are esteemed by God. In light of the fact God has counted us valuable, we go forward. David had to learn at a difficult moment of his life that he had nothing to prove. When you already have the promises of God, you need nothing else. Oh, I admire David's courage, but he was operating from the wrong premise. When you know God's promises, you don't have to prove anything.

WHEN YOU KNOW GOD'S FAITHFULNESS, YOU DON'T HAVE TO FEAR ANYTHING

If you examine this time in David's life, you'll see that he begins to vacillate. He gets confused between what he believes and how he behaves. It is as though he is saying, "I believe one thing, but I'll live something else." All of us are like that at times, not living out what we know to be true. David had been doing fine with King Saul, until a new war broke out with the Philistines. "And there was war again: and David went out and fought with the Philistines, and slew them with a great slaughter; and they fled from him" (1 Samuel 19:8). Once again David proved himself victorious, but that just irritated King Saul all the more.

> And the evil spirit from the Lord was upon Saul, as he sat in his house with his javelin in his hand: and David played with his hand. And Saul sought to smite David even to the wall with the javelin; but he slipped away out of Saul's presence, and he smote the javelin into the wall: and David fled, and escaped that night (1 Samuel 19:9–10).

This time David ran home to be with his wife, Michal, but Saul sent spies to watch for him. Recognizing her father's trickery, Michal warned David to escape, helped him flee through a window at night, then pulled some of her own trickery on her father by putting a dummy in her bed.

Now one might think that David and Michal were just being shrewd, but the fact is they both manipulated their circumstances instead of putting their trust in God. A few weeks earlier, David had stood up to a giant with no support system at all except a slingshot and the name of God. Now he's at home, hiding from a handful of spies, and he sneaks off into the night. David wasn't trusting in the faithfulness of God. His wife told lies about the entire event. Rather than trusting in the plan of the Lord, they are creating their own plans.

We have a record of exactly what David was feeling at this time, for Psalm 59 tells us it was written by David "when Saul sent and they watched the house to kill him." That Psalm clarifies the difference between what David felt and what he believed:

> Deliver me from mine enemies, O my God: defend me from them that rise up against me. Deliver me from the

workers of iniquity, and save me from bloody men. For, lo, they lie in wait for my soul: the mighty are gathered against me; not for my transgression, nor for my sin, O Lord. They run and prepare themselves without my fault: awake to help me, and behold. Thou therefore, O Lord God of hosts, the God of Israel, awake to visit all the heathen: do not be merciful to any wicked transgressors. Selah.

They return at evening: they make a noise like a dog, and go round about the city. Behold, they belch with their mouth: swords are in their lips: for who, say they, doth hear? But Thou, O Lord, shalt laugh at them; Thou shalt have all the heathen in derision. Because of his strength will I wait upon Thee: for God is my defense. The God of my mercy shall prevent me: God shall let me see my desire upon mine enemies. Slay them not, lest my people forget: scatter them by Thy power; and bring them down, O Lord our shield. For the sin of their mouth and the words of their lips, let them even be taken in their pride: and for the cursing and lying which they speak. Consume them in wrath, consume them, that they may not be: and let them know that God ruleth in Jacob unto the ends of the earth. Selah.

And at evening let them return; and let them make a noise like a dog, and go round about the city. Let them wander up and down for meat, and grudge if they be not satisfied. But I will sing of Thy power; yea, I will sing aloud of Thy mercy in the morning: for Thou hast been my defense and refuge in the day of my trouble. Unto Thee, O my Strength, will I sing: for God is my defense, and the God of my mercy.

It is evident from these words of David that he understood that God is faithful and will protect His own, but he wouldn't trust in it and live it out. Instead, he chose to live in fear. That's a shame, for David was the one man who should have understood that God is faithful and will protect His own. Instead, David ran to see Samuel. When Saul's soldiers showed up at Samuel's place to arrest David, they couldn't do it. The Spirit of God came upon the whole group, and they started prophesying, everybody forgot the purpose of their errand. Those soldiers returned to Saul, who sent a fresh group of soldiers to pick up David, and the same thing happened. He did it a third time, and again the Spirit came upon the soldiers of Saul. Finally the king himself decided to come, and the same thing happened to him. Saul started prophesying, and joined in with everybody else, and David was able to escape. You see, if

David had trusted in God's faithfulness from the start, he wouldn't have had to run around quite so much. God would have protected him. David's support system was not to be found in hiding places and chicanery, but in the power of God.

When Martin Luther was being hunted down by the Roman prelates for his stand during the Reformation, some friends hired a fortress overlooking the Rhine and put him inside for safe keeping. After a few days, Martin Luther left that hideout, for he was tired by seeking protection from a human fortress. Instead, he went back into the cities, with no protection at all, and wrote a wonderful hymn: "A mighty fortress is our God, a bulwark never failing." Rather than trusting in human devices, Luther was trusting in God. He understood that the Lord is faithful, so we don't have to fear anything.

WHEN YOU KNOW GOD'S FELLOWSHIP, YOU CAN HANDLE LOSING A FRIEND

God was trying to make David totally dependent on Himself, to prepare him for the difficult days he would face as a king. In allowing these tough times to occur, God had at least provided one close friend in the person of Jonathan. I think it's one of the great friendships in all literature. Jonathan went to his father to plead for his friend David's life. But Saul, sick with jealousy and anger, not only wanted to kill David, he even attempted to murder his own son. Jonathan raced out to warn David to stay away, and the two friends hugged each other and wept in sorrow.

Consider all the difficulties David was facing. He had once had a great relationship with King Saul, but that was now totally destroyed due to Saul's jealousy and envy. David had a rich relationship with Jonathan, but that was now taken away, as the two friends would no longer be able to see each other. Even David's relationship with Michal was largely gone, due to her father's actions toward her husband. God isolated David from everyone, taking away all his relationships. All those he could once rely upon were now gone. David would have to be solely dependent upon God for his strength, for there was no one else left.

Please don't misunderstand me. I recognize that there was pain and disappointment in David's life. I'm sure he didn't enjoy this time in his life. None of us appreciates the hard times we go through. We cannot underestimate the pain of a long illness, or a wayward child, or a failed marriage. But as the Lord taught David, when we know God's fellowship, we can handle even the loss of a friend. God is enough, even though we go through heartbreak and hard times. Sometimes the only way we can learn that is by reducing our helps to God alone. We can look upon our discouragements and disappointments and say, "One thing I know for sure: God was with me."

APPLICATION

1. When have you suffered with self doubt?

   a. What helped pull you through that period?

   b. What advice would you have for a fellow believer who said, "I just don't feel worthy of God"?

2. Why do you think there has been such an emphasis on self-esteem in our society?

   a. What are people really seeking when they attempt to improve the way they feel about themselves?

   b. What is the source of self-esteem for a Christian?

3. What was David trying to prove by killing 200 Philistines?

a. What's wrong with that mentality?

b. The first point in our study was "When You Know God's Promises, You Don't Have to Prove Anything." What promises has He made that grant us such security?

4. Look over Ephesians 1:1–14. What does Paul say the Lord has done for us?

a. What further evidences does Paul refer to in Ephesians 2?

b. What comfort or encouragement do these truths offer your life?

5. When have you found yourself believing one way, but living another?

a. What does Psalm 59 reveal about the way David was thinking, and how does that contrast with the way he was acting?

b. What should David have done differently?

6. On what grounds can you trust in the faithfulness of God?

a. How can a Christian build his or her faith in God?

7. Why did the Lord allow all the friends to be pulled from David's life?

a. How would you have responded in the situation?

b. How has God worked to develop your trust in Him?

DID YOU KNOW?

Michal, the youngest daughter of Saul, was David's first wife. Though she apparently loved David, her mocking of him on one occasion (2 Samuel 6:16–22) may have resulted in the end of their intimacy, for she never had children (2 Samuel 6:23). In an attempt to strengthen his house against the house of Saul, David took foreign wives, each of whom bore him a son in Hebron (2 Samuel 3:1–5). After returning to Jerusalem, he took even more concubines and wives (2 Samuel 5:13), in direct violation of God's prohibitions for kings in Deuteronomy 17:17. The disastrous results of David's worldly marriage practices would come back to haunt him in the latter part of his reign (2 Samuel 13–19; 1 Kings 1–2).

REACHING AN ALL-TIME LOW

1 Samuel 21–22

In this lesson we will discover how to learn from our mistakes and lean on the Lord.

OUTLINE

When David was being pursued, he made the mistake of not trusting in God. He had to scheme to protect his life, lie to cover up his plan, and degrade himself before his enemies in order to save himself. David's lack of faith not only led to despair and discouragement, it put the lives of other people in danger. In this chapter we will examine the mistakes David made, and explore some lessons we can learn.

I. David Was Defiled Before Ahimelech

II. David Was Degraded Before Achish

III. David Was Delivered Before Adullam

IV. Lessons from David's Life

They said he was a Christian. He had done a great deal of work for the Lord. He had founded ministries and funded them with his own money. He was a successful businessman in the community, with a wife and family, known for helping others in need. But financial difficulties began to take over his empire. He owed a great deal of money. Eventually he took out a large insurance policy on his wife, conspired with two underworld characters, and arranged to have her kidnapped and murdered. When the plot began to unravel, no one could believe the rumors. How could an upstanding Christian man be involved in something so evil? But it was true, a jury found him guilty, and today that man is serving time in prison.

Some would argue that he couldn't really be a Christian, but the fact is we are all sinners. Any individual, even a person who knows God, can become entrapped in evil. The capacities of an individual to stray from his moorings in the faith are astounding. Yet every time we hear about a believer falling into sin, we ask the same question: "How could it happen?"

The life of David is a perfect example. There are no depths too low for a man to sink if he breaks fellowship with God and begins to walk in the flesh. I have watched Christians assassinate one another with their tongues, deliberately cause divisions in the church, and even embezzle money from other believers. Believers who get out of fellowship with God can do some pretty terrible things. So don't be surprised to find that the same man anointed king over Israel got into a lot of trouble. None of us can stand in righteousness on our own—we all need desperately to cling to Christ.

David had tried to prove his worth to God by killing two hundred Philistines, he had developed his own plan for running away from Saul, and he had forgotten to trust the Lord. David knew about the faithfulness and promises of God, but he failed to put them into practice. So after spending some time with the prophet Samuel, he fled to a place called Nob, where three things happened.

DAVID WAS DEFILED BEFORE AHIMELECH

Then came David to Nob to Ahimelech the priest: and Ahimelech was afraid at the meeting of David, and said unto him, "Why art thou alone, and no one with thee?" And David said unto Ahimelech the priest, "The king hath commanded me a business, and hath said unto me, 'Let no man know any thing of the business whereabout I send thee, and what I have commanded thee: and I have appointed my servants to such and such a place. Now therefore, what is under thine hand? Give me five loaves of bread in mine hand, or what there is present." And the priest answered David, and said, "There is no common bread under mine hand, but there is hallowed bread; if the young men have kept themselves at least from women." And David answered the priest, and said unto him, "Of a truth women have been kept from us about these three days, since I came out, and the vessels of the young men are holy, and the bread is in a manner common, yea, though it were sanctified this day in the vessel."

So the priest gave him hallowed bread: for there was no bread there but the showbread, that was taken from before the Lord, to put hot bread in the day when it was taken away. Now a certain man of the servants of Saul was there that day, detained before the Lord; and his name was Doeg, an Edomite, the chiefest of the herdmen that belonged to Saul. And David said unto Ahimelech, "And is there not here under thine hand spear or sword? For I have neither brought my sword nor my weapons with me, because the king's business required haste." And the priest said, "The sword of Goliath the Philistine, whom thou slewest in the valley of Elah, behold, it is here wrapped in a cloth behind the ephod: if thou wilt take that, take it: for there is no other save that here." And David said, "There is none like that; give it to me" (1 Samuel 21:1–9).

So it was a late Friday afternoon, the day before the Jewish Sabbath, when David and a few followers arrived in the village of Nob. Running from an angry King Saul, they decided the priest Ahimelech and the peaceful village of 86 people was a perfect place to hide. It was off the main drag, had few visitors, so hosting the king's son-in-law and his entourage must have been quite an event. The people obviously didn't expect much trouble, since there was only one sword in the entire village, but Ahimelech noticed that David wasn't with a royal party, and he asked what was happening. That's where David started getting into trouble. In essence he said, "I'm on a secret mission for the king." It was a bold-faced lie, for David was running from the king, not representing him! He was a fugitive, not an ambassador.

David hadn't had time to grab any provisions before hitting the road, so he asked for food and was told all the priest had were the five loaves of bread meant for the sacrifice. He offered them to David and his men. There was nothing wrong with taking the bread, as Jesus would point out years later, but there *was* something wrong in deceiving the priest. David lied to set up a false scenario, and his lie came back to haunt him. When we walk in our own wisdom, neglecting the leadership of the Lord, we set ourselves up for problems. Lying complicates life, and David's was about to get extremely complicated. I once heard a man say, "Always tell the truth, that way you'll never have to remember what you said to whom."

David had lost his focus on God, and in trying to protect himself got further into trouble. Had he been walking with God, this entire affair never would have happened. Instead of trusting in the provision and protection of God, the anointed king of Israel was hiding out and lying to priests.

DAVID WAS DEGRADED BEFORE ACHISH

David next asked Ahimelech for a weapon by telling another lie: he had started his secret mission so quickly, he'd forgotten to bring his sword. So Ahimelech handed David the only sword in the city—the one that had belonged to Goliath. Upon seeing it, David strapped it on, then headed out to find another hiding place, this time in the city of Gath.

Unfortunately, Gath had been Goliath's home. So here was David, the guy who had killed the giant, running away from King Saul and seeking refuge in the giant's hometown, wearing Goliath's sword on his belt. As you can imagine, his entrance into the city caused quite a stir. David must have expected that people had forgotten his battle with the giant, since years had passed. He thought he could walk into the city, lose himself, and take sanctuary there. David was wrong.

Achish, the king of Gath, immediately found out about it:

And the servants of Achish said unto him, "Is not this David the king of the land? Did they not sing one to another of him in dances, saying, 'Saul has slain his thousands, and David his ten thousands?'" And David laid up these words in his heart, and was sore afraid of Achish the king of Gath (1 Samuel 21:11–12).

Apparently that hit song about David had been heard in Gath, and nobody there liked it. Here was David, actually wearing Goliath's huge sword around his waist, so the people of Gath didn't have too much trouble making the connection. They took a good look at him and said, "Hey—that's David!"

When we walk in our own wisdom, we really complicate our lives. David had lied to Ahimelech, had taken the only weapon in town, and that very weapon put him in grave danger. This was perhaps the lowest point in his life to that time, for now he not only feared Saul's soldiers but the townspeople all around him. Recognizing he wasn't exactly among friends, David decided he had to do something quick. "So he changed his behavior before them, pretended madness in their hands, scratched on the doors of the gate, and let his saliva fall down on his beard" (verse 13 NKJV). In other words, David began to slobber all over himself. He flailed around, banging his hands against the city gate, acting like he was crazy. Here is the sweet singer of Israel, the man after God's own heart, banging his head against the wall and drooling on himself to try to weasel his way out of trouble. You never can tell what a person will do when they fall out of fellowship with God. They can do the strangest things possible, losing all sense of propriety. The anointed king of Israel was totally degraded, having to act like a madman just to save his own skin!

I love Achish's response: "Ye see the man is mad: wherefore then have ye brought him to me? Have I need of madmen, that ye have brought this fellow to play the madman in my presence? Shall this fellow come into my house?" (verses 14–15). In other words, Achish was saying, "This guy is a crackpot! I don't want some lunatic in my house—he might be dangerous!" David must have felt awfully low at that point, having to pretend he was crazy in order to save his own skin. If only he had trusted God, none of this sort of degradation would have happened.

DAVID WAS DELIVERED BEFORE ADULLAM

Again running for his life, David decided the only safe place would be a cave:

> David therefore departed thence, and escaped to the cave Adullam: and when his brethren and all his father's house heard it, they went down thither to him. And every one that was in distress, and every one that was in debt, and every one that was discontented, gathered themselves unto him; and he became a captain over them: and there were with him about four hundred men (1 Samuel 22:1–2).

So this is where all David's scheming led him: in a cave, surrounded by 400 unhappy, debt-ridden, sometimes crazy people. These were desperate men—a group that would grow to 600 and turn into a group called "David's Mighty Men." But at that time they were little more than rabble.

It was in that cave, surrounded by losers, with time to reflect on his situation, that David was delivered. We have some poems he wrote while he was hiding in that cave, and they reveal his heart as David decided it was time to repent and put his trust in God. In Psalm 57, which the text says was written "when he fled from Saul in the cave," we have these words:

> Be merciful unto me, O God, be merciful unto me: for my soul trusteth in Thee: yea, in the shadow of Thy wings will I make my refuge, until these calamities be overpast. I will cry unto God most high; unto God that performeth all things for me. He shall send from heaven, and save me from the reproach of him that would swallow me up. Selah. God shall send forth His mercy and His truth. My soul is among lions: and I lie even among them that are set on fire, even the sons of men, whose teeth are spears and arrows, and their tongue a sharp sword. Be thou exalted, O God, above the heavens; let Thy glory be above all the earth. They have prepared a net for my steps; my soul is bowed down; they have digged a pit before me, into the midst whereof they are fallen themselves. Selah (Psalm 57:1–6).

David had been hunted, discouraged, and degraded. He was caught up in his own devices, and eventually wound up in a cave, surrounded by people with as many problems as he had. He was isolated, at the end of his rope, when suddenly he realized his problem: He needed to get back with God. So he called out to the Lord in prayer. Charles Spurgeon once noted that "if David would have prayed in the palace like he prayed in the cave, he never would have run in the first place." But by letting his behavior move away from his beliefs, David got caught up into some serious trouble. That's a perfect illustration of what can happen when we move away from God.

THE LESSONS OF DAVID

As I've reflected on this chapter in David's life, I can see at least three important applications we can make. First, when we are out of fellowship with God, we inevitably seek bad counsel. At the start of all these troubles, David was with the prophet Samuel. God had worked through that prophet, saving David from Saul's soldiers and from Saul himself. David was right there beside that man of God, and he failed to ask his counsel. Instead, he chose to run away, eventually surrounding himself with malcontents and misfits. I've seen that pattern again and again, as people get out of fellowship with God. They start heading down the wrong path, and inevitably seek counsel from the wrong people—often people who don't know the Lord. Countless times people in crisis have told me they asked the advice of a non-Christian friend, rather than seeking godly counsel. I've found myself talking to couples experiencing marital difficulties, they're about to divorce, and when I ask them who they've been talking to about their problems, they'll inevitably name a secular counselor. Some couples have told me the marriage counselor advised a divorce in their very first session together! When we're not walking with God, we take counsel from the wrong people.

Second, when we are out of fellowship with God, we make bad choices. David was supposed to be the wise king of Israel, but he chose to walk around Goliath's home town with the giant's sword on his belt. It often seems that people who have started walking away from the Lord have stopped using their heads. If we're not walking close to God, we get out of touch with His wisdom. We start making poor choices in our ignorance.

Third, when we are out of fellowship with God, we set in motion bad consequences. One of the overlooked characters in David's journey is a man named Doag. He was an Edomite who found out that David had visited the city of Nob. Doag told King Saul about it, and Saul got so angry that he gathered the entire village together and instructed his footman to kill them all. The footman refused to slaughter a priest, but then Doag pulled out his sword and started hacking away. Remember, the people of Nob didn't have any weapons, since they'd given the only sword to David. They couldn't defend themselves, so Doag killed 85 of them—men, women, and children. One man, Abiathar, escaped and told David what had happened. When David found out about it, he said to Abiathar, "I have occasioned the death of all the persons of thy father's house" (1 Samuel 22:22). David's foolish actions had unintended consequences.

David hadn't intended to get anyone killed; but in straying out of fellowship, he set in motion a disaster. By being deceitful and trying to arrange his own plan, he set in motion a chain of events that led directly to the slaughter of 85 innocent people. Imagine the sorrow he experienced the rest of his life over that mistake. David invited Abiathar to stay with him, and I imagine every time David looked upon that man, he felt guilty. When we wander away from God, we can set in motion a chain of bad consequences. But if we walk closely with the Lord, trusting in His plan and protection, we'll save ourselves much heartache and trouble. God is faithful, and we must remember to rely on Him at all times.

APPLICATION

1. When you are faced with danger, what is your first reaction:

screaming	running away	freezing up
calling for help	fighting back	acting tough
getting mad	praying	breaking into tears

2. As you look at this period of David's life, what would you say were his biggest mistakes?

   a. Why do you suppose he didn't ask Samuel's advice?

   b. What do you think Samuel might have told him?

3. When have you asked someone else for advice in a difficult situation?

   a. Who do you like to turn to for advice? Why?

b. Why is it important to turn to a fellow believer for advice?

4. Was it wrong for David to lie to Ahimelech to protect his own life? Why or why not?

   a. How did David's action lead to the murder of the people of Nob?

5. Did God forgive David for his actions? If so, then why didn't the Lord take away the consequences?

   a. What's the difference between being forgiven and living with the consequences of our sin?

   b. How would you respond to a young girl who said to you, "My boyfriend got me pregnant. I prayed for God to forgive me for my sin! Why would He let this happen?"

6. David had to resort to feigning madness and sleeping in a cave, surrounded by malcontents. What do you suppose he was feeling in those situations?

a. What do Psalms 57 and 142 reveal about the things David learned?

b. What lessons do those Psalms offer us?

7. Take the time to write your own psalm, based upon the things you've learned from your own mistakes.

DID YOU KNOW?

Once, on the Sabbath, Jesus and His disciples were walking through a grain field ready for harvest (Matthew 12:1–8). The disciples were hungry and were picking and eating some of the ripe heads of grain. Some Pharisees accused Jesus of allowing His disciples to break the law—actually, a Jewish tradition outlawing harvesting on the Sabbath, based on Exodus 34:21. Jesus used the example of David eating the showbread from the Tabernacle, given to him by the priest, Ahimelech, at Nob. Technically, the showbread was only to be eaten by priests (Leviticus 24:9). Jesus used the illustration of Ahimelech's compassion to show that the Law was given to serve man, not vice versa; that compassionate acts are always within the scope of God's law.

A PRAYER
FROM A CAVE

1 Samuel 22:1–2 & Psalm 142

*In this lesson we will learn how to turn
our problems into praise.*

OUTLINE

As David sat in that cave, contemplating what had gone wrong in
his life, he decided to write out his feelings in a psalm. His words
capture the intense depression he suffered, but they also present a
plan for moving out of that depression and toward a new attitude
in the Lord. This chapter will explore the lessons of David's prayer
from the cave.

I. **Life in a Cave Is the Pits**
  A. Disoriented
  B. Deserted
  C. Depressed
  D. Defeated

II. **From Problems to Praise**
  A. Verbalize the Problem Before God
  B. Visualize the Problems Before God
  C. Realize the Power and Provision of God
  D. Arrive at the Place of Victory

The life of David is a great encouragement to all of us because he mirrors the expressions and feelings of our own hearts. David was a man of faith and a man of vision, but he also was a man who sometimes struggled with putting his faith into practice. For example, after running away from King Saul, seeking refuge in places like the small village of Nob and the enemy territory of Gath, David found himself sitting in a cave, contemplating his life. This is a representative experience for many of us. There are times each of us has a "cave experience," where we find ourselves out of touch with God and facing a difficult situation brought on by our own mistakes. To try to get a handle on his problems, David wrote poetry. This was a way to get his thoughts down on paper, express his heart toward the Lord, and reveal to us the working of God in David's life.

In 1 Samuel 22:1–2 we read:

> David therefore departed thence, and escaped to the cave Adullam: and when his brethren and all his father's house heard it, they went down thither to him. And every one that was in distress, and every one that was in debt, and every one that was discontented gathered themselves unto him; and he became a captain over them: and there were with him about four hundred men.

Most scholars believe that King Saul levied a heavy tax upon the inhabitants of Israel; and many of these people left discontented and in debt, were the victims of high taxation, struggling for their very existence. Many were no doubt old friends of David who had decided to join him after hearing of his exile. As word got out, others decided to join them, for the next chapter reveals that their numbers grew to 600. They were the debtors, the distressed, and the discontented—David must have been like Robin Hood, leading a ragtag group of rebels.

As he sat in that cave, David had plenty of time to think about his walk with God. He probably went into the cave to be alone. He wanted to get away from everyone. Instead he found himself surrounded by the distressed of Israel. He took a hard look at his life, and it caused his poetic side to come out. David wrote eight different psalms while he was running from King Saul, and I'm glad he spent so much time writing, for his words help me comprehend what was going through his heart at the time.

Life in a Cave Is the Pits

As you read through the words of Psalm 142, you'll be able to see the condition of David's soul.

Disoriented

First, he was *disoriented*. He says in verse 3, "When my spirit was overwhelmed within me . . ." The Hebrew words in the phrase literally mean, "in the muffling of my spirit." His spirit was so wrapped up in troubles and gloom, so muffled with woe, that his powers of judgment were weakened. In other words, David felt like a fierce flood had rushed upon him. He could barely stand up against the flow, like a man struggling to walk against a strong current. He was overwhelmed and disoriented.

We've all felt that way at times. When I come home from a long trip and see my desk stacked high with papers, I will sometimes just sit down and stare at the pile, feeling lost in the weight of responsibilities and expectations. That's similar to what David was feeling, only his disorientation was even greater. He was being hunted by the king, surrounded by the hurting, so encumbered with problems that he didn't know what to do first. David was also burdened with guilt over unintentionally causing the deaths of everyone at Nob, and felt the weight of responsibility for all those around him who saw him as their leader. Have you ever felt that disoriented? Have you sat in that cave? Then you know what David was feeling.

Deserted

Second, he felt *deserted*. "I looked on my right hand, and beheld, but there was no man that would know me: refuge failed me; no man cared for my soul" (verse 4). Even though there were people all around David, he felt alone; he felt there was nobody who cared for him.

Problems have a tendency to isolate us. We build a shell around ourselves, thinking we are the only ones with problems. The more we think about it, the more certain we are no one else understands. I think about times I wanted to talk with someone about the pressures of pastoring, or the difficulties of being a father, wondering if I was the only one facing those struggles. That's exactly how David felt while sitting in that cave.

Depressed

Third, he felt *depressed*. "I am brought very low," he writes in verse 6. David used the Hebrew word for depression or indentation, equating it with his feeling about himself. I've counseled many depressed people, and I know what a heavy burden it is to feel low. I've known people who have ended their own lives because of the feeling of despair they had for their future. They look around the world, see the problems, and decide it's not worth fighting any more. David was depressed like that. All his hope and joy were gone. The thoughts of his problems had turned inward, so that King Saul's chase wasn't the trouble so much as David's own emotions were the trouble.

Christians sometimes mistake depression for sin, but I enjoy reading about the great preachers of history, and I'm overwhelmed at the number of great pastors who have struggled with depression. Charles Spurgeon used to get so depressed he would have to take months away, just to be by himself and not think about the pressures of ministry. The prophet Elijah experienced tremendous depression. So did Jonah and Moses. Many of God's people have felt like giving up, seeing no hope in the midst of their troubles.

Defeated

Fourth, he felt *like giving up.* David continues in verse 6, "Deliver me from my persecutors, for they are stronger than I." He had made a score sheet for all his problems, listing all his persecutors on one side and failing to come up with any names for the other side. He even asked God to "bring my soul out of prison" in verse 7, feeling incarcerated by all his troubles. This is the low point of David's life, and he is sharing his honest feelings. He is alone, dejected, defeated, and overwhelmed. I can identify with him, for I've had some low points in my own life. Maybe you can too. But the good news is that David doesn't stay in that low spot—he works his way out of it.

FROM PROBLEMS TO PRAISE

It's impossible to read Psalm 142 and not notice the author's depression. But it is imperative that we understand how David moved from depression to praise. He starts out saying, "I cried unto the Lord," but he ends up saying, "for Thou shalt deal bountifully with me." How did he move from dejection to confidence?

Verbalize the Problem Before God

First, he verbalized the problem in his life. I like reading this psalm often, because it reminds me of all the things I don't like to do when I have problems. As you look at the words of David, he says things like:

- "I cried out unto the Lord" (verse 1).
- "I poured out my complaint" (verse 2).
- "I cried unto Thee, O Lord" (verse 5).
- "Attend unto my cry" (verse 6).

David tells God how he is feeling. He describes what is going on inside him. Why is it so hard for us to do that? When we have problems, even overwhelming problems that are bigger than we can bear, we need to tell the Lord. When we speak our minds fully, name the problems and people that plague us, it is like revealing a secret to our best friend. God is there, and He cares about us. We can tell Him anything that's in our hearts, like a true friend to whom we pour out our hearts.

There are times when everybody needs a buddy, with whom we can get in the car, roll up the windows, and start venting. You can scream and holler and cry if you want, knowing the other person will accept you. Some people may not think that sounds very spiritual, but unless you get to the place where you can honestly tell God what you're feeling, you'll be stuck with it bottled up inside you. I don't mean we have to complain or be negative, but sometimes we just have to cry out from the cave.

For example, one of my favorite writers was Joe Bayly, a man who experienced a number of terrible tragedies. He lost three children in three separate accidents, and wrote a book called *A View from the Hearse* in which he described his pain. In one poem, he spoke of traveling the country as a speaker, all alone, with no one to talk to, laugh at his jokes, listen to his complaints, or even say his name correctly. Sure, he was feeling sorry for himself, but he was also verbalizing what was happening in his life. By verbalizing it, he was better able to understand it.

When David expressed his pain to God, it was not only the confession of a problem, but a clarification of the problem, and an admission that he needed God's help. If you're going through so many hard things that you don't know if God still cares, tell Him all about it. Verbalizing the problem is the first step toward healing.

Visualize the Problem Before God

Second, he visualized the problem before God. "I showed before Him my trouble," David writes in verse 2. It is as though David drew a picture of the problem, laying it out for the Lord to see. I believe one of the dangers we have in praying is that we rush into requests before spending time in praise. Jesus revealed a pattern for praying that we ought to follow, for in His pattern worship comes before requests. If we do not praise God, we will not be able to fully reveal our problems to Him. The purpose of praise is to reveal God as worthy—praise has a tendency to make God big in our hearts, so that when we start talking about our problems, we pour them out to a mighty God who is able to do something about them. David didn't just complain about being depressed, he visualized his problems before the awesome God of creation.

When Moses sent twelve spies to check out the Promised Land, ten came back and complained of obstacles. But Joshua and Caleb, stubborn men of faith, reminded the people that they had a big God. The ten saw their problems in respect to their own resources, and were frightened. But the two saw the problems in light of God's resources, and were encouraged. The best thing we can do when sitting in a dark cave of depression is to spend time praising God, then laying out the problem before Him.

Realize the Power and Provision of God

Third, he envisioned the power and provision of God. In verse 3, David started recognizing something important about the Lord: "When my spirit was overwhelmed within me, then Thou knewest my path." As David talked about his problems, he began to remember God's provision and problem-solving ability. He remembered that God already knew all about his troubles. David was speaking to one who understands. "Thou art my refuge and my portion in the land of the living," he writes in verse 5. In other words, as David talked through the issues, he began to see God for who He is. As David revealed how he felt, and visualized the problem before the Lord, he began to understand that God knew what he was feeling.

Arrive at the Place of Victory

Fourth, he arrived at a place of victory. "Bring my soul out of prison," we read in verse 7, "that I may praise Thy name; the righteous shall compass me about, for Thou shalt deal bountifully with me." In thinking through the issues and revealing them to the Lord, David moved from problems to praise. He came to discover that God can be trusted in times of danger. He came to see God's power as being greater than his problems. I imagine the mood of that cave must have changed over night. One voice began singing praises to God, until it swelled into a chorus of 600 voices, all offering praises to the Lord most high.

APPLICATION

1. Read Psalm 6. How does David describe his trouble?

   a. What does he ask God to do for him?

   b. What does he ask God to do for his enemies?

2. Read Psalm 7. How is David's trust evident in the psalm?

   a. What encouraging words does he use?

   b. How do you see *praise* taking precedence over *problems* in this psalm?

3. Read Psalm 25. What does this psalm teach us about God?

   a. What does it reveal about David's attitude?

   b. Which verses would you like to make your prayer?

4. Read Psalm 56. What happened to bring about the creation of this psalm?

   a. What specifically does David accuse his enemies of doing?

b. What promises does David make?

5. Read Psalm 69. What does David admit in this psalm?

a. How does he verbalize his problems?

b. What lessons do you take from this psalm for your own life?

6. Read Psalm 142. Why is verbalizing a problem important?

a. How does praise help us move toward victory?

b. What solution does David arrive at?

DID YOU KNOW?

The many months David spent fleeing from Saul was undoubtedly an emotional time, and David found release during that period of anguish and separation by writing—journaling, if you will. We know of at least eight psalms he penned during that period, as evidenced by the notes in the titles of the psalm: Psalm 18, praise for deliverance from Saul; Psalm 34, when he pretended to be insane before Abimelech; Psalm 52, when Doeg informed on David's whereabouts to Saul; Psalm 54, when the Ziphites revealed David was hiding among them; Psalm 56, when the Philistines seized him in Gath; Psalm 57, when he hid from Saul in the cave; Psalm 59, when Saul posted sentries to keep watch for David; and Psalm 142, another reflection while hiding from Saul in the cave. Journaling proved a powerful way to invoke God's presence in David's day-to-day affairs.

HOW TO TREAT YOUR ENEMY

1 Samuel 24

In this lesson we will learn how to mend a broken relationship.

OUTLINE

Once, while Saul was chasing David all over the country trying to kill him, David was given an opportunity to take revenge. His response to that moment gives us a model we can follow in restoring broken relationships.

I. **Refuse Revenge**

II. **Risk Reconciliation**

III. **Restore the Relationship**

OVERVIEW

I watched a famous football coach get fired not long ago—dumped because he lost to a traditional rival. It was interesting to watch his response. First, there was a sense of resignation. He seemed to accept his firing as part of big-time college football. After a few days, however, you could hear a sorrow in his voice. He was saddened over what had happened. But then his tone changed, and in interviews he began to sound like a man bent on revenge. Of course, as often happens, the entire affair ended up in court, with the team agreeing to pay him a big sum, and both sides agreeing not to criticize the other in print.

We seem to be living in an age when people want to resolve everything by going to their lawyers. Suing people has become the great American pastime. There are 22,000 lawsuits filed every day in the United States, which is about twenty times higher than in Japan, and more than ten times as many as European nations. So extensive is our attempt at revenge that we have even developed the concept of "rent-a-judge," where people can find an arbitrator, rent him for a day or two, and help solve the dispute out of court. It's cheaper, and you don't have to wait for months like you do in the clogged court system. Revenge is simply big business today. It's also something most of us have to deal with at some point in our lives. How do we deal with life when we have been wronged? What do we do when people mistreat us? If we listen to the voices in our culture, we'll take them to court. But if we listen to the Word of God, we'll see that He has a different plan.

David was a man who had every right to take revenge on Saul. King Saul was extremely jealous of David, and had continued to hunt him with his soldiers. It raised such a ruckus that the Philistine army thought it would be a good time to attack again, in hopes that Saul would be too distracted with David to bother battling them. Saul had to regroup, pull his soldiers together to protect Israel from attack, and that allowed David to escape to Engedi, a rough place with many caves and hiding places. A fugitive, David had known just about every indignity imaginable: he had lied to others, hidden in a cave, feigned insanity, been separated from his best friend and from his wife, and had resorted to leading a band of marauders. He must have been deeply hurt by Saul's actions. If any man had a right to revenge, it was David—after all, the Lord had already anointed him king over Israel. He had done nothing to deserve such shabby treatment from Saul. David had ministered to Saul, obeyed his orders, done everything asked of him, and his reward was to become the target of Saul's wrath.

So great was Saul's intense hatred of David, that as soon as the fighting with the Philistines died down, Saul immediately began his pursuit. David and his 600 men were being chased by Saul and his 3,000 soldiers. And the Bible reveals what happened when David was confronted with the opportunity to seek vengeance. So as we explore this passage of Scripture, think about the times you have been mistreated. If you had it in your hands to return evil to them, knowing you would not be punished, what would you do?

REFUSE REVENGE

"Then Saul took three thousand chosen men out of all Israel, and went to seek David and his men upon the rocks of the wild goats. And he came to the sheepcotes by the way, where was a cave; and Saul went in to cover his feet: and David and his men remained in the sides of the cave." (1 Samuel 24:2–3). King Saul was out trying to find David, so that he could kill him, when he heard the call of nature. There were no restrooms around, so the king went into a cave to relieve himself. Unknown to Saul, David was hiding in that very cave. At that point, David had opportunity to take revenge on his enemy. He could have reasoned that "God delivered Saul into my hands." The possibility that Saul would choose the exact cave where David was hiding was remote, so David could have said to himself, "This is what I've been praying for. God must have given me this opportunity!" He could have taken his revenge right there.

Instead, David offered us a principle for dealing with those who have hurt us: Refuse revenge when circumstances seem to allow for it. David didn't immediately assume that just because Saul had wandered into his cave, the Lord arranged it so David could take revenge. Instead, he kept himself from taking advantage of a timely opportunity.

"And the men of David said unto him, 'Behold the day of which the Lord said unto thee, Behold, I will deliver thine enemy into thine hand, that thou mayest do to him as it shall seem good unto thee'" (verse 4). The second principle I see in this episode is this: Refuse revenge when counselors advise it. The men with David didn't like Saul, for the king had put them into debt and distress. I can just hear them whispering, "Here's our chance, David! God arranged this. Kill him! Get this over with. We're tired of living in caves." I find that evil men often try to use God as an excuse for their own sin. I've seen men who don't know God at all using His truth to promote their own ideas. They're a dangerous breed, for they want to use the counsel of God without the Spirit of God. David could have been swayed by them, listening to them say that "God had arranged" for him to kill Saul. But David refused. Instead, "David arose, and cut off the skirt of Saul's robe privily" (verse 4). Thinking no one was in the cave, Saul had taken off his robe while about his business; and David quietly crept forward, took a knife, and cut off the edge of Saul's robe. David never said a word, and Saul didn't know it had happened.

It's interesting that after David did cut Saul's robe, he was sorrowful. The chapter is a good testimony to the sensitive heart of the young man, for his conscience was smitten: "And it came to pass afterward, that David's heart smote him, because he had cut off Saul's skirt" (verse 5). He knew he shouldn't have done that to the king of Israel. David hadn't taken full revenge, but he had taken advantage of an opportunity to make the king look silly. He had listened to his counselors enough to do something that would be a measure of revenge.

The opportunity to take revenge on Saul was there. His counselors were encouraging him to do it. But David would not, and that was the right course of action. It may seem like "getting even" with someone will make things better, but it seldom does. The Bible tells us that vengeance is wrong. You only end up hurting yourself. By not taking Saul's life, David allowed his case to be tried in the courts of heaven. He refused to take action on behalf of God. As Solomon once put it, "Say not, 'I will do so to him as he hath done to me': I will render to the man according to his work" (Proverbs 24:29). We are to refuse revenge, for God is the one who will take vengeance on those who have wronged us.

RISK RECONCILIATION

If I'm having a problem with someone, the Bible says it is my responsibility to go to them and seek reconciliation. But most people won't go that route because it is risky. There are risks practically every step of the way. To begin with, it may not work. I can make an effort to restore the relationship, and have all my words thrown back in my face. There is also the risk that I'll say the wrong thing, which would only make the problem worse. There is the risk that my analysis of the entire situation is wrong, so that by risking reconciliation I am only exacerbating the problem. So when David determined to try to get things right with Saul, he was taking a risk.

Two things are clear in this passage. First, David risked the ridicule of men. Verse 6 tells us that, after recognizing he had done the wrong thing, David said to his men, "The Lord forbid that I should do this thing unto my master, the Lord's anointed, to stretch forth mine hand against him, seeing he is the anointed of the Lord." The next verse goes on to say that David "suffered them not" or restrained his men with his words. The word literally means "tore apart." In other words, David had an argument with his own men. Their counsel was clear: "Kill Saul." David's answer was just as clear: "No, that would be wrong."

David was taking a big risk by saying no. He was risking that the men might say he'd lost his nerve. They might accuse him of being weak, or of not dealing with his problems. But David stuck by what he knew was right. I think peacemakers are often viewed as weak, but it takes a strong person to risk reconciliation. A man is never weak when he stands upon the principles of God's Word. David would not be swayed to take the wrong action, even though his own followers were encouraging him to do so. He knew what God wanted him to do, and was willing to stick by it. His courage must have shown through, for he swayed his men to change their minds, and they did not lift their hand against Saul. David risked the ridicule of men in order to bring about reconciliation.

Second, David risked the retaliation of Saul. The next few verses in the chapter reveal that after Saul went out of the cave, David came out behind him and cried out, "'My lord the king!' And when Saul looked behind him, David stooped with his face to the earth, and bowed himself" (verse 8). The king must have been startled to see his enemy behind him, and realized immediately that David had been in the cave with him. David was risking that Saul would immediately send his soldiers after him, but he was willing to risk retaliation because he wanted to seek reconciliation.

There is a stunning confrontation that occurs in front of that cave, and it offers us a wonderful model for reconciling with an enemy. First, David presents the facts. "And David said to Saul, 'Wherefore hearest thou men's words, saying, "Behold David seeketh thy hurt"? Behold, this day thine eyes have seen how the Lord hath delivered thee today into mine hand in the cave: and some bade me kill thee: but mine eye spared thee, and I said, "I will not put forth mine hand against my lord; for he is the Lord's anointed!"'" (verses 9–10). David doesn't try to dodge around the problem, nor does he get all emotional about it. He simply lays out the facts by telling Saul he is listening to the wrong people. They were lying to Saul. David had never been the king's enemy.

I've often seen relationships strained because a third party got involved and offered some bad information. I've seen friends estranged because somebody heard something hurtful and felt they had to pass it on. Many relationships on the body of Christ have been broken due to bad information, and that's what happened to Saul.

Next, David proves his faithfulness. He held up the corner of the robe that he'd cut off and said, "Moreover, my father, see, yea, see the skirt of thy robe in my hand: for in that I cut off the skirt of thy robe, and killed thee not, know thou and see that there is neither evil nor transgression in mine hand, and I have not sinned against thee; yet thou huntest my soul to take it" (verse 11). David could have killed Saul. He had the opportunity, if he'd wanted to take it. The corner of the robe was proof of that. David laid out the facts, offers evidence of his faithfulness, and then pledges his friendship by saying, "The Lord judge between me and thee, and the Lord avenge me of thee: but mine hand shall not be upon thee" (verse 12). In other words, David had no plans to harm Saul, and his restraint in the cave proved it. "The Lord therefore be judge, and judge between me and thee, and see, and plead my cause, and deliver me out of thine hand" (verse 15).

In seeking to reconcile, David presented the facts, proved his faithfulness, and pledged his friendship. Those are the same three things we ought to do if there is someone with whom we want to reconcile. Sometimes people have heard bad information, and all they need is a clear understanding of the situation, and the affirmation that we are not their enemy, and reconciliation will take place.

RESTORE THE RELATIONSHIP

And it came to pass, when David had made an end of speaking these words unto Saul, that Saul said, "Is this thy voice, my son David?" And Saul lifted up his voice, and wept. And he said to David, "Thou art more righteous than I: for thou hast rewarded me good, whereas I have rewarded thee evil. And thou hast shown this day how that thou hast dealt well with me: forasmuch as when the Lord had delivered me into thine hand, thou killedst me not. For if a man find his enemy, will he let him go well away? Wherefore the Lord reward thee good for that thou hast done unto me this day" (verses 16–19).

Confronted with outright grace and righteousness, the only thing Saul could do was cry. He saw David's integrity, and, for the moment, repented of his own behavior. I think at that moment Saul recognized that David was going to be the next king of Israel. It was the moment of truth for Saul. He even went on to say, "And now, behold, I know well that thou shalt surely be king, and that the kingdom of Israel shall be established in thine hand" (verse 20). Saul's character didn't change, and his repentance would be short-lived, but in that one moment, he saw David to be a man after God's own heart. He knew David would replace him as king.

"Swear now therefore unto me by the Lord, that thou wilt not cut off my seed after me, and that thou will not destroy my name out of my father's house. And David sware unto Saul. And Saul went home; but David and his men gat them up unto the hold" (verses 21–22). After acknowledging that David should be king, Saul asked for the protection of his children. Saul was a selfish man, who should have been pleading forgiveness rather than asking favors, but all he wanted was to protect his own house. And David, a truly gracious man, obliged. Years later he would take care of Mephibosheth, Saul's crippled grandson.

Of course, if Saul just wanted to negotiate, David could have done the same thing. He could have said, "Well, I'll take care of your kids, if you'll stop chasing me around these rocks." But perhaps he knew that asking for Saul's word on anything was a waste of time. The interesting thing in this passage is that David forgave Saul, restored the relationship, and even made a promise to protect Saul's name in the future. Saul didn't promise anything. He didn't even change. But that didn't stop David from doing all he could to restore the relationship.

When we are in similar situations, we should follow David's example. If your spouse has done something to hurt you, forgive. That's your responsibility. Don't insist they change. David was not responsible for Saul's behavior, but for his own, and God used this to prepare him to be a better king. I am called to forgive my brother, even if I suspect he will hurt me again. That's what David did. He refused revenge, risked reconciliation, and restored the relationship. Imagine how our lives would change if each of us followed that pattern.

APPLICATION

1. Why doesn't the Lord want us to take revenge?

   a. How did David refuse revenge?

   b. What do you think would have been the result if he had taken revenge?

2. What counsel did David get from others?

3. What did David do to restore his relationship with Saul?

a. What response did it elicit from Saul?

b. What should you do if you try to restore a relationships and the other person refuses to change?

4. Read Psalm 7. What is David's attitude about himself? About his enemies? About God?

a. With whom are we to leave our disputes?

b. What does this psalm reveal about God?

5. What is the pattern of restoration given in Matthew 18:15–18?

a. Who takes the first step?

b. What if the other person doesn't respond?

DID YOU KNOW?

When Christians have unresolved conflicts with one another, they are often tempted to take their disputes before a civil (non-Christian) court in the form of a lawsuit. The apostle Paul severely rebuked the Christians in Corinth for doing just that (1 Corinthians 6:1–11). In order to keep believers from going to court against one another (for the reasons mentioned by Paul), several ministries now provide arbitration services for believers which will hopefully lead to a resolution of their conflict. Ministries such as the Christian Mediation and Arbitration Service and Peacemaker Ministries match Christians with a qualified arbitrator who applies biblical principles to the conflict. (Contacts may be made by searching for their web sites on the Internet.)

DAVID AND ABIGAIL

1 Samuel 25

*In this lesson we will see how one wise woman
saves two men from sin and death.*

OUTLINE

David had to learn that vengeance remains in the hands of God.
Once, when a fool showed his great disrespect, David planned to
take action. Instead, David was restrained by the godly behavior of
the fool's wife. This chapter will take a look at that story, and the
lessons it has for all of us.

   I.   **The Foolish Farmer**

  II.   **The Furious Soldier**

 III.   **The Faithful Wife**

 IV.   **The Lessons of Abigail's Life**

Throne word spread rapidly throughout Israel: Samuel the prophet was dead. The man who had judged the nation and given Israel her first king was gone. All Israel gathered together to lament his passing. As soon as the funeral was finished, David headed for the wilderness of Paran, south of Judah. This area was often the target for Philistine and Amalekite raids, and mercenaries were often hired to provide protection for the shepherds. One of the farmers who had land in that area was a man by the name of Nabal. David protected his people and watched over them. The shepherds close by claimed that David's men "were very good to us, and we were not hurt, neither missed we any thing, as long as we were conversant with them, when we were in the fields. They were a wall to us both by night and day, all the while we were with them keeping the sheep" (1 Samuel 25:15–16). Of course, there was a reciprocal agreement in this action. The soldiers would protect the farmer's men, and in return the farmers would provide food, shelter, or clothing as needed.

So it was quite natural that David brought ten of his men into the area, and instructed them to visit Nabal.

> And thus shall ye say to him that liveth in prosperity, "Peace be both to thee, peace be to thine house, and peace be unto all that thou hast. And now I have heard that thou hast shearers: now thy shepherds which were with us, we hurt them not, neither was there aught missing unto them, all the while they were in Carmel. Ask thy young men, and they will show thee. Wherefore let the young men find favor in thine eyes; for we come in a good day: give, I pray thee, whatsoever cometh to thine hand unto thy servants, and to thy son David" (verses 6–8).

It was shearing time; the time when farmers paid those who had helped them, so David had sent ten men with a gracious message to Nabal. David's men had contributed to Nabal's prosperity, so it was only fair that they receive something for their assistance. Notice that David didn't set a price, but asked only to be paid whatever was thought fair. But what happened next presents a picture of people and their attitudes toward others. There are three main characters, and we need to examine each of them.

THE FOOLISH FARMER

When David's men arrived to talk with Nabal, they were not received warmly.

> And Nabal answered David's servants, and said, "Who is David? And who is the son of Jesse? There be many servants nowadays that break away every man from his master. Shall I then take my bread, and my water, and my flesh that I have killed for my shearers, and give it unto men, whom I know not whence they be? (verses 10–11)

Nabal was not a gracious man. He was very wealthy, owning property, 3,000 sheep, and 1,000 goats. He had set up a shearing time for all those sheep, normally a time of celebration and festivity. Nabal was having none of that.

He was not only wealthy, he was wicked. Verse 3 describes him as "the man was churlish and evil in his doings." The word "churlish" is translated "harsh" in the New King James version. He was obnoxious and unreasonable, flaunting his prosperity. Nabal was an ugly person. His employees hated him. One of his servants described him as "for he is such a son of Belial, that a man cannot speak to him" (verse 17). His own wife refers to him as a man of Belial—literally a "son of the devil" (verse 25). She even went so far as to say, "for as his name is, so is he: Nabal is his name, and folly is with him."

The Hebrew word *nabal* actually means "fool," so apparently Nabal's wife thought he lived up to his name! In the context of the Old Testament, to be a fool didn't mean to be a man who was stupid or ignorant. It meant a man lived his life apart from God, trying to do things his own way, without regard for anyone else. It was a way of destruction, and that's exactly what Nabal was like. He was a fool—a wicked man.

There are Nabals everywhere in our world today; churlish men who cannot say thanks for anything, who cheat others, and who make life miserable for everyone. Nabal had been greatly helped by David and his men, but rather than respond in gratitude, he suggested that David and David's men were probably causing an uprising against Saul. He knew exactly what David's men had done for him, but he didn't want to give up any of his precious money so he accused David of something evil. He was truly a foolish farmer.

The Furious Soldier

When David's men returned and repeated Nabal's response, David became furious. He said to his men, "Gird ye on every man his sword" (verse 13), and he took 400 men to see Nabal. Now you don't put on your sword to have a meeting. You put on your sword because you're going to war. David was angry, and he meant to do something about it. "Surely in vain I have kept all that this fellow hath in the wilderness, so that nothing was missed of all that pertained unto him: and he hath requited me evil for good." (verse 21). David was going to kill Nabal, then kill all of Nabal's men.

Perhaps David had a tendency to over-react when angry. That's a common response. When Saul got mad at David, he sent 3,000 soldiers to capture him. When David got mad at Nabal, he took 400 soldiers with him. He was seething at the disrespect.

You can imagine what was going through David's mind on his trek to see Nabal. He was replaying the evil words the man had spoken, and getting more and more angry as he thought about their innuendo. He must have been thinking, "I've had enough! Who does this guy think he is? I did everything possible to help this character, and he treats me like dirt. Nobody messes with me like that!" It's funny, but I've found myself thinking those same thoughts on occasion. All of us have gotten angry at the way someone treated us, and we start gearing up for battle in our minds. David was one furious soldier.

The Faithful Wife

That's when Abigail, Nabal's wife, entered the scene. She was one of the most wonderful women in Scripture, one of the unsung heroines of the Old Testament. A faithful wife, she heard about what had happened and determined to deflect the anger of God's servant in order to stop him from making a terrible mistake. Her wisdom shines through in this story.

There are several things that set Abigail apart. First, she was a good woman. Verse 3 tells us that Abigail was "a woman of good understanding, and of a beautiful countenance." The words "good understanding" mean she was wise, and later verses reveal she could speak the truth. So as David was preparing for a battle, Abigail was preparing for peace. After hearing from a servant about her husband's foolish actions, she prepared a feast, sent it to

David, then went out to meet him. She was wise, knowing that you cannot treat a man like David, the anointed king, with disrespect.

Second, she was a gracious woman. As you read what she does, you can see her gracious spirit. "And when Abigail saw David, she hasted, and lighted off the ass, and fell before David on her face, and bowed herself to the ground, and fell at his feet, and said, 'Upon me, my lord, upon me let this iniquity be: and let thine handmaid, I pray thee, speak in thine audience, and hear the words of thine handmaid'" (verses 23–24). As you read through her speech, you'll find she refers to David as "lord" eight times. She uses the word "please" several times. She bows down before David, showing him her utmost respect. She points out that had she seen David's servants, rather than her husband, she would have given them what they wanted. Abigail was everything Nabal was not— reminding us that you don't have to become like the person you live with. Though Abigail lived with a negative, churlish man, she became a positive, gracious woman.

Third, she was a gallant woman. I'm overwhelmed at her bravery. Here was a band of 400 angry soldiers coming after her husband, and her response was not to run, but to do the right thing. She gave David a wealth of food, then pleaded for her husband's life, not knowing how David would respond to her. Keep in mind that he had already expressed his intention of killing everybody, so Abigail had no way of knowing if David would take his anger out on her. She courageously took the initiative to stop his anger and save her husband's unworthy life.

Fourth, she was a godly woman. Everything about her suggests that Abigail was a woman who loved God. Certainly the servants recognized that, for they came to her with the news of David's arrival, rather than to her husband. And as she gave her speech to David, to try to stem his anger, she said, "I pray thee, forgive the trespass of thine handmaid: for the Lord will certainly make my lord a sure house; because my lord fighteth the battles of the Lord, and evil hath not been found in thee all thy days" (verse 28).

Abigail had heard about David's victory over Goliath, recognized that he was in partnership with God, and knew the Lord was with him. She not only knew about David's faithfulness to God, but she was certain of God's faithfulness to David: "Yet a man is risen to pursue thee, and to seek thy soul; but the soul of my lord shall be bound in the bundle of life with the Lord thy God; and the souls of thine enemies, them shall he sling out, as out of the middle of a sling" (verse 29). In other words, Abigail knew that David's life was secure in God, and that his enemies would be tossed out like the stone he had flung at Goliath.

Abigail went on to say,

> And it shall come to pass, when the Lord shall have done for my lord according to all the good that He hath spoken concerning thee, and shall have appointed thee ruler over Israel; that this shall be no grief unto thee, nor offense of heart unto my lord, either that thou hast shed blood causeless, or that my lord hath avenged himself: but when the Lord shall have dealt well with my lord, then remember thine handmaid (verses 30–31).

Abigail, a godly woman, knew that God would remain faithful. She reminded David that one day he would be king of Israel, and when he took the throne he didn't need some petty grievance bothering his conscience. The actions of Nabal weren't worth a bad conscience. My friend, that is godly counsel. Abigail was candid with David, reminding him of the future. She knew that God was faithful, but she also recognized that sin is faithful to remind us of our failings.

David certainly appreciated her words. His first response was, "Blessed be the Lord God of Israel, which sent thee this day to meet me: And blessed be thy advice, and blessed be thou, which hast kept me this day from coming to shed blood, and from avenging myself with mine own hand" (verses 32–33). So David took her advice, accepted her gift, and sent her home in peace. That wise, godly woman not only saved her husband's life, she stopped David from making a mistake. She was a tool in the hands of the Lord to accomplish His purpose.

The Lessons of Abigail's Life

When Abigail got home, you might think she would receive some thanks, perhaps even some encouragement. Instead, for saving his life, she got grief: "And Abigail came to Nabal; and, behold, he held a feast in his house, like the feast of a king; and Nabal's heart was merry within him, for he was very drunken: wherefore she told him nothing, less or more, until the morning light" (verse 36). Instead of being able to celebrate her good work, she had to deal with a drunken fool. She waited until the morning to tell her husband what she had done. "But it came to pass in the morning, when the wine had gone out of Nabal, and his wife had told him these things, that his heart died within him, and he became as a stone" (verse 37).

What David thought he had to do for himself, the Lord did on his behalf. Vengeance is God's, not ours. When word got back to David that Nabal had died, he realized the Lord's work on his behalf. He celebrated the fact that God had been faithful. David understood that Abigail had saved him from making a big mistake, that the Lord had dealt with the problem, and he was happy that God had once again proven Himself faithful.

There is one other thing that occurred: "And David sent and communed with Abigail, to take her to him to wife" (verse 39). He recognized her wisdom and godliness, and knew he would appreciate a woman like that in his life. And Abigail didn't think about it for a minute—after all those years with a scoundrel, she just raced out to join a man after God's own heart.

As I read this story, I am reminded that a man who lives his life without God is a fool. The wages of sin is death, so Nabal reaped exactly what he sowed. If a man is determined to live for himself, he can expect a sad and lonely exit from this world. He may think he can live his life selfishly, but sooner or later it will catch up to him. Of course, I am also reminded that we don't have to become like Nabal just because we live with him. There's an old adage which says, "If you live with someone long enough, you become like them." That may be true at times, but it is also possible to *not* be like them. Abigail teaches us that it is possible for a woman to maintain her spirit of love and graciousness even though married to a churlish fool. I think it's instructive that Abigail never puts down her husband. She is candid about him, but remember that she was still out there trying to faithfully support him. Difficult as it was, she was faithful, and God honored her for her faithfulness.

Though David had a chance to take revenge on Saul, he chose not to. Though he had a chance to take revenge on Nabal, he chose not to. In both cases he came close to doing something he would long regret. Apart from God's faithfulness, we are doomed to repeat our mistakes. Apart from His faithfulness, we are destined to reproduce the failures of others. The very thing Saul did to David, David was now trying to do to someone else. God gave David a way of escape, reminding him through a godly woman that anger and revenge are destructive.

He offers us that same escape. If you are angry with someone, give up that anger. Learn from the life of David, and trust in the faithfulness of God.

APPLICATION

1. What had David asked Nabal for?

   a. Why had he asked?

   b. Was it a fair request?

2. How did Nabal respond?

   a. Was that a fair response?

   b. When has someone responded that way to you?

   c. How did you handle it?

3. What do you think made Nabal into the kind of man he was?

   a. Why did he respond to David the way he did?

   b. Who have you known who is like Nabal?

4. What was David's first response?

   a. When have you felt that same way?

   b. Why are anger and vengeance so destructive to our lives?

5. What words come to mind when you read about Abigail?

a. Who have you known who is most like Abigail?

b. What sets them apart from others?

6. If a friend of yours was married to a churlish fool, what advice would you give her?

a. What helps you maintain a positive attitude in a difficult situation?

7. Who are you most like: Nabal, David, or Abigail? Why do you say that?

a. What lesson from this lesson is most meaningful to you?

DID YOU KNOW?

Abigail employed the wisdom expressed in Proverbs 26:4: "Do not answer a fool according to his folly, lest you also be like him." Even though David was in the right, he would have become a fool like Nabal if he had reacted in anger. This counsel of Abigail is consistent with the words of Jesus centuries later, "Do not give what is holy to the dogs; nor cast your pearls before swine . . ." (Matthew 7:6). However, the very next verse in Proverbs, 26:5, seems to say the opposite: "Answer a fool according to his folly, lest he be wise in his own eyes." When you answer in anger, you become like the fool, but if you answer with wisdom, you set him straight. It takes the discernment of Abigail to know what to do, and when.

DAVID'S DEEP DEPRESSION

1 Samuel 27 & 30

In this lesson we will learn how to overcome depression.

OUTLINE

David, tired of being chased by Saul daily, eventually gave in to his depression. Rather than listening to God, he listened to the voice in his head that told him to quit. He moved away from Israel, and at the same time moved away from God. In this chapter we will study how David fell into such a state, and what he did to get out of it.

I. **The Circumstances of Depression**
   A. An Enemy He Could Not Master
   B. An Expectation He Could Not Meet

II. **The Cost of Defection**
   A. Deceiving Himself
   B. Dishonoring God
   C. Destroying His Testimony
   D. Descending into Further Sin

III. **The Control of Deceit**
   A. Discouragement Leads to Defection
   B. Depression Dictates the Depth of Life
   C. God Delivers Endless Encouragement

W hy is it that success often brings discouragement rather than elation? Many men and women of God throughout history who have reached the pinnacle of success have found themselves facing depression. In David's case, some of his most morose moments were captured in his songs. In Psalm 10:1 he asks, "Why standest Thou afar off, O Lord? Why hidest Thyself in times of trouble?" In Psalm 13:1 we read, "How long wilt thou forget me, O Lord? Forever? How long wilt thou hide thy face from me?" And in Psalm 22:1 he writes, "My God, My God, why hast Thou forsaken me?" Those are the words of a discouraged man. They are also words that reveal the heart of David.

THE CIRCUMSTANCES OF DEPRESSION

In 1 Samuel 27:1, we find the reason for such discouragement in David. Saul had once again been trying to kill him, and in despair David reasons, "I shall now perish one day by the hand of Saul: there is nothing better for me than that I should speedily escape into the land of the Philistines; and Saul shall despair of me, to seek me any more in any coast of Israel: so I shall escape out of his hand." He was tired of running, tired of fighting, and tired of feeling like an enemy in his own country. David had two reasons for being depressed.

An Enemy He Could Not Master

Saul's hatred for David ran deep, and the king had once again been trying to hunt him down. In chapter 26, David had discovered Saul's camp, and instead of killing his persecutor, had taken Saul's sword and water jug. Then he stood on a nearby hilltop and chided the king's guard for doing such a lousy job of protecting the king. "And now see where the king's spear is, and the cruse of water that was at his bolster" (1 Samuel 26:16). Once again David could have killed Saul, but he refused to do so.

He should have been encouraged when the king asked his forgiveness, but he knew too well that Saul's jealousy was terminal, that the king would never repent, and would go to his grave hating David. The Bible tells us that Saul "sought him every day," so the pressure must have been tremendous. David's last thought as he went to bed each night must have been about the hatred his king felt for him. It was a constant burden, something from which David could find no release.

Sometimes the enemies we cannot master are our constant companions. If you have a long term illness, the burden of it weighs heavily on your soul. If you're facing an insurmountable problem, it seems to bother you all the time, intruding upon your thoughts at all hours. Satan is like that, trying to discourage and defeat us. The Bible says that our struggle is not against flesh and blood, but against the spiritual forces of evil. So it was for David. His enemy was constantly on his mind, working for his destruction, disturbing his peace. He had an enemy he could not master.

An Expectation He Could Not Meet

David had taken up a great responsibility. Six hundred men and their families relied upon his leadership, and their concerns also burdened his heart. In addition to being hunted on the outside, he was loaded down with pressures from inside his own camp. So David decided to give up.

Knowing the king would always hate him, David decided to leave Israel altogether: "And David arose, and passed over with the six hundred men that were with him unto Achish, the son of Maoch, king of Gath. And David dwelt with Achish at Gath, he and his men, every man with his household, even David with his two wives, Ahinoam the Jezreelitess, and Abigail the Carmelitess, Nabal's wife" (1 Samuel 27:2–3). With all the pressures and all the stress, David just decided he couldn't handle it any more. He walked away from Israel, giving in to the influences of the world.

I think we've all felt like doing that at one time or another. Sometimes the pressure can blur the focus of our lives. For example, think of all the people who have grown to hate the pressures and expectations of Christmas—a time when we should be rejoicing! But we feel the pressure to attend all the parties, the housewarmings, the presentations, the programs, dinners, desserts, and meetings, in addition to responding to all the cards and calls, until we feel like saying, "I give up!" I heard about a woman in a department store, burdened with packages, tired children hanging on her, and as she waited for an elevator she complained out loud, "Whoever started this Christmas thing ought to be shot!" To which a voice behind her said, "Too late, lady . . . they already crucified Him." Suddenly her perspective on Christmas was put back into focus.

You may have an enemy you cannot master. You may have expectations you cannot reach. Pressures have a way of getting us out of focus, and that's exactly what happened to David. Rather than praying, rather than seeking godly counsel, he just gave in to his feelings and decided to call it quits.

THE COST OF DEFECTION

David decided to give in to the enemy. He defected, moving to the area of the Philistines. The price he paid in making that sort of decision was steep. There are a number of problems with his decision to join the enemy.

Deceiving Himself

Word came to King Saul that David had gone to Philistia, and the king gave up the chase. There was no more reason to hunt David. Saul had been jealous that David would one day inherit his throne, but David could not take the throne as long as he was living in Philistia. David had become part of the enemy.

Of course, David thought that by doing so the pressure would be off, but that was merely a self-deception. The fact that Saul was no longer chasing him didn't make David safe. He had defected to Gath, the homeland of Goliath, filled with people who had opposed David his entire life.

Running away from a problem is no way to solve it. Some people look for peace in a bottle, or a pill box, or by killing the pain with drugs. These cause a kind of peace, but it is a deceiving sort of peace. They create a false sense of security. While they may have deadened themselves to outward pressure, the inward pressure remains. In a day or a week, when they awaken from their stupor, they will look at the same old world and the same old pressures they had before. In running to Philistia to find peace, David deceived himself.

Dishonoring God

David was God's anointed, strategically selected by the Lord to lead Israel. Samuel the prophet had confirmed his anointing, and Jonathan, King Saul's own son, had agreed to it. Even Saul himself had admitted that David was to replace him as king over Israel. Yet David believed Saul's threat to kill him. He doubted God's confirmed promise. The man who had once written of God being his light and salvation, who had asked, "The Lord is the strength of my life; of whom shall I be afraid?", and who had claimed, "Though an army may encamp against me, my heart shall not fear," was now doubting the word of God. David denied his Lord, refusing to believe the promise of the Almighty. All of us, if we look at our circumstances rather than the Word of the Lord, can do the same. When we leave God out of our lives, all the brightness and hope disappears. David chose on that dark day to believe in his circumstances rather than in the Lord. In doing so he dishonored God.

Destroying His Testimony

Philistia was a land full of idols and wicked priests. The Philistine people were not God's people, nor their land God's land. What kind of an influence would that place have on David's family, on his men, and on their wives and children? A careful study of Scripture reveals that the roots of rebellion in David and his men trace back to the decision to move to Philistia and settle in the city of Ziklag.

Descending into Further Sin

Think about all the problems David created for himself. He had to find a way to take care of all his men, so they began raiding nomadic tribes and other establishments and stealing their food: "And David and his men went up, and invaded the Geshurites, and the Gezrites, and the Amalekites" (1 Samuel 27:8). Eventually they had to kill people to get things: "And David smote the land, left neither man nor woman alive, and took away the sheep, and the oxen, and the asses, and the camels, and the apparel, and returned, and came to Achish" (verse 9). The reason they killed everyone was to leave no witness to the crimes.

David then had to start lying to king Achish, claiming that his men were raiding Israel: "And Achish said, 'Whither have ye made a road today?' And David said, 'Against the southern area of Judah' . . . David saved neither man nor woman alive, to bring tidings to Gath, saying, 'Lest they should tell on us, saying, So did David,' and so will be his manner all the while he dwelleth in the country of the Philistines" (verses 10–11). And Achish believed David's lies, saying, "He hath made his people Israel utterly to abhor him; therefore he shall be my servant forever" (verse 12). Achish thought that David would be forced to be his ally. The stealing, murder, and lies continued, all because David had allowed depression to control his life.

THE CONTROL OF DECEIT

Discouragement Leads to Defection

David's discouragement led him to defect. In doing so, he descended into the depths of sin. I don't think depression is a sin, but we cannot allow it to lead us into sinful behavior. David allowed the pressure to defeat him, and he defected from God. The Bible says that he lived in this condition for sixteen months, walking apart from God.

Depression Dictates the Depth of Life

When we face depression, we cannot allow it to dictate how we will live. When we are depressed, we ought never to listen to ourselves. A discouraged man is his own worst enemy. When we're down, we talk negatively to ourselves. In reviewing all the bad things in his life, David began to believe Satan's lie that there was no hope for his future. But in descending into sin, David created more problems than he'd had before.

God Delivers Endless Encouragement

One day, while David and his men were out marauding, the Amalekites came and attacked Ziklag. They took the women and children captives, stole the provisions, and burned the city to the ground. When David's group returned, they found nothing but a charred mess. At that moment, everyone turned on David. The Bible reveals his men were about to stone him. That's when David finally woke up. First Samuel 30:6 reads, "And David was greatly distressed; for the people spake of stoning him, because the soul of all the people was grieved, every man for his sons and for his daughters: but David encouraged himself in the Lord his God." Instead of trying to solve things himself, David finally turned back to God. That's the solution for anyone facing depression and discouragement.

When it seems like everything is pressing in on us, when we have enemies we cannot master and expectations we cannot meet, we do not have to defect. We can cast ourselves upon the Lord. We can read His promises, accept His comfort, and receive His encouragement. When we read the promises of God in the Bible, we can't help but be encouraged at the reminder that God has always taken care of His people. As we speak with Him in prayer, we begin to sense His leading in our lives. The very moment we feel least like praying is when it is most important to pray. We have a God who is never overcome by our circumstances, but makes us overcomers in Jesus Christ. No matter how dark the circumstances may first appear, He is with us, powerful and able to see us through the darkest days.

APPLICATION

1. Where do you go to feel close to God?

    a. What do you do to hear to His voice and sense His direction in your life?

    b. What is the one thing that helps you the most when you are discouraged?

2. In your own words, what caused David to defect?

    a. What pressures do you have in your life that push you toward "defecting" from the faith?

b. What expectations are put upon you that you feel you cannot meet?

3. When in your life have you felt the closest to the Lord?

a. When have you felt the farthest away?

b. What steps did you take to move back toward Him?

4. Why do Christians face so much discouragement?

a. How does giving in to discouragement lead directly to sin?

b. In what ways have you felt pressured to compromise?

5. Who is the most encouraging person you know?

a. Who encourages you in your Christian life?

b. Who have you been encouraging?

6. How can reading the Bible help a discouraged believer?

   a. What passages of Scripture encourage you the most?

   b. How do you pray when you are discouraged?

DID YOU KNOW?

If there was a time in David's life when he lived as a "prodigal," this was it. Like the famous prodigal son in Jesus' story (Luke 15:11–32), who one day simply "came to himself" (or "came to his senses," NIV, verse 17), David woke up to the foolishness of his lifestyle and turned back to God. After the Amalekites plundered Ziklag, David left for Hebron where the Judahites anointed him king. According to 1 Chronicles 4:30–31, David incorporated into Judah the territory of Simeon where Ziklag was located, bringing it under his protection. Was this an act of restitution consistent with David's repentance, an attempt to bless those whom he had taken advantage of? If so, it is evidence of David's "coming to his senses."

TWO MEN IN MISERY

1 Samuel 28 & 29

*In this lesson we will solve the mystery of misery—
how to turn it into joy!*

OUTLINE

Every time we move away from God, we move toward trouble.
David had moved away, and it landed him in the middle of the
enemy camp. Saul had moved away, and it cost him his kingdom.
Where the lives of these two men intersect, we find a lesson about
the importance of remaining close to God.

I. **The Misery of David**
   A. The Deception
   B. The Dishonesty

II. **The Misery of Saul**
   A. The Fear
   B. The Failure
   C. The Fall

III. **The Intervention of God**

IV. **The Lessons of David and Saul**

The Bible, like all good stories, presents the truth in dramatic form. For years, "Perry Mason" has intrigued people with his ability to discern the unsolvable mystery. One of the interesting things about the stories is that you cannot follow them if you come in the middle of the plot. You have to be there from the beginning, for the entire plot contains points and counterpoints that you won't understand unless you see the whole thing. Perry puts all the little pieces together, one at a time, until it all comes together in the courtroom.

The story of Saul and David is like that. You'll find part of it in one chapter, part in another, and there are little pieces all through the book of 1 Samuel. Suddenly at the end, it all comes together. The two plot lines join together, resolving the entire story. David, in despair, had given up on Israel and moved into Philistia with his men. Turning his back on the truth, he decided God was no longer able to take care of him. The result was that David became involved in sin. Like all men, David had character flaws. He had a tendency toward dishonesty. When things weren't looking good, David resorted to lies and deception. He had his wife Michal lie for him, he persuaded Jonathan to lie for him, and David himself lied to the priest Ahimelech, Achish the king, and King Saul. Lying seems to have been David's besetting sin. It had led him into an intolerable situation—living with the enemy, apart from Israel.

THE MISERY OF DAVID
The Deception

The dilemma David faced is apparent in the following verses:

"And it came to pass in those days, that the Philistines gathered their armies together for warfare, to fight with Israel. And Achish said unto David, 'Know thou assuredly, that thou shalt go out with me to battle, thou and thy men.' And David said to Achish, 'Surely thou shalt know what thy servant can do.' And Achish said to David, 'Therefore I will make thee keeper of mine head forever'" (1 Samuel 28:1–2).

David thought he had simply hidden himself with the Philistines. But now the king who had offered him protection was expecting David to join forces and attack Israel. Poor David! If he refused Achish, he would be in deep trouble in the place where he was living. And if he accepted Achish's request, he would be in even worse trouble in Israel. The future king of Israel was asked to fight his own people. He could be either a liar or a traitor. There was no right answer.

The Dishonesty

David was so involved in intrigue, deception, and dishonesty, he was now expected to join the enemy. When we ask the world for help, we can expect to pay their price at some point. David had asked Achish for help, and now Achish was asking for help in return. David's answer was a rather vague reply. He didn't say, "I can't fight my own people," instead muttering, "you know what I can do." Achish took that to mean David was volunteering. He believed David promised to help, taking it as a statement of loyalty, and made David captain of his personal guard.

Think of the misery David must have been going through. He was expected to attack his own people, marching in front of the Philistine army where everyone from Israel could see him. But if he refused, Achish would surely send all his soldiers after him. David was in deep trouble. But then, just as we reach this dramatic point, the story shifts.

THE MISERY OF SAUL

David wasn't the only man in misery. The King of Israel was also going through some misery of his own.

> "Now Samuel was dead, and all Israel had lamented him, and buried him in Ramah, even in his own city. And Saul had put away those that had familiar spirits, and the wizards, out of the land. And the Philistines gathered themselves together, and came and pitched in Shunem: and Saul gathered all Israel together, and they pitched in Gilboa. And when Saul saw the host of the Philistines, he was afraid, and his heart greatly trembled" (1 Samuel 28:3–5).

The Fear

Consider the fear of Saul. The Philistines, recognizing that Israel's godly leader, Samuel, was dead, decided it was time to attack Israel. Having rebelled against God, Saul felt fear born from a lack of trust and a guilty conscience. He could no longer call on the Lord because he had despised the prophet Samuel, murdered the priests of Nob, and hunted God's chosen leader David. He had every reason to be afraid. Here was Saul, facing major problems, completely unable to turn to God. He was out of fellowship, living in sin, and didn't know what to do.

The Failure

Next, think about the failure of Saul. "And when Saul inquired of the Lord, the Lord answered him not, neither by dreams, nor by Urim, nor by the prophets" (verse 6). Those are some of the saddest words in Scripture. Saul tried praying, but he had waited too long. There was no repentance or confession, and his prayer wasn't heard. Remember, the prophet Isaiah warns us to "seek ye the Lord while He may be found, call upon Him while He is near." Saul had waited too long, and his sin had created a wall between himself and God. He had lived a life of rebellion, and the Lord was not going to be used like a genie in a bottle just because Saul was now facing a crisis.

Too many people think they can ignore God their entire lives, then call upon Him at the last moment and expect an answered prayer. The fact is, our relationship with God today influences the efficacy of our prayers tomorrow. The Psalms tell us that if we hold iniquity in our hearts, God will not hear our prayers, and Saul's heart was filled with iniquity. He had unconfessed sin, had no desire to change, and was only running to the Lord at the last minute because he could think of no other scheme to try.

I've known people who were living in sin, and knew they were in disobedience to God, but announced they would ask God to forgive them later. That's not how God works. First Chronicles 10 reveals that Saul never really inquired of the Lord. He asked for help, but he didn't really pray. If he had prayed, he would have been down on his knees, weeping out his confession of sin, and begging the Lord to forgive and change him. God never heard Saul's prayer. It never reached His ears.

The Fall

Now consider the fall of Saul. In 1 Samuel 28:7 we read that Saul said, "Seek me a woman that hath a familiar spirit, that I may go to her, and inquire of her." This same guy who, a few verses earlier, had "put the mediums and spiritists out of the land" was now calling for a séance! Since Saul couldn't talk with God through prayer, he decided to talk with God through a witch. A woman in Endor was famous for holding séances, so Saul dressed in a disguise, went to visit her, and asked her to bring up a spirit. He even assured her that "as the Lord liveth," she wouldn't get in trouble for doing it! Saul had absolutely no morals left at all.

The witch held her séance and apparently the prophet Samuel appeared.

> And when the woman saw Samuel, she cried with a loud voice: and the woman spake to Saul, saying, "Why hast thou deceived me? For thou art Saul!" And the king said unto her, "Be not afraid: for what sawest thou?" And the woman said unto Saul, "I saw gods ascending out of the earth." And he said unto her, "What form is he of?" And she said, "An old man cometh up; and he is covered with a mantle." And Saul perceived that it was Samuel, and he stooped with his face to the ground, and bowed himself (verses 12–14).

Now there are various ways to understand this passage. Some people think the whole thing was a trick foisted upon Saul by the witch. Others believe she really caused Samuel to appear. But what I believe happened is that God made Samuel to appear, for the Lord says in Ezekiel 14:7–8:

> For everyone of the house of Israel, or of the stranger that sojourneth in Israel, which separateth himself from Me, and setteth up his idols in his heart, and putteth the stumbling block of his iniquity before his face, and cometh to a prophet to inquire of him concerning Me; I the Lord will answer him by Myself: and I will set My face against that man, and will make him a sign and a proverb, and I will cut him off from the midst of My people; and ye shall know that I am the Lord.

In other words, God will respond in anger to His people who seek out familiar spirits.

What Saul did was a terrible violation of the Word of God. The Bible forbids divination and seeking spirits. Whatever happened, the message Saul received was terrible:

> And the Lord hath done to him, as he spake by me: for the Lord hath rent the kingdom out of thine hand and given it to thy neighbor, even to David: because thou obeyedst not the voice of the Lord, nor executedst His fierce wrath upon Amalek, therefore the Lord hath done this thing unto thee this day. Moreover the Lord will also deliver Israel with thee into the hand of the Philistines: and tomorrow shalt thou and thy sons be with me: the Lord also shall deliver the host of Israel into the hand of the Philistines (1 Samuel 28:17–19).

Samuel pronounced a harsh judgment on Saul, and anyone who thinks he can find a shortcut to God by consorting with wizards will face the same message of doom and judgment. Saul was in misery, and resorted to evil to try to find his way out, but the prophet could only speak of more misery.

THE INTERVENTION OF GOD

Though the Lord was unwilling to intervene in Saul's life, He was still willing to intervene in the life of David. Though he had never been willing to raise his hand against King Saul, David was now being numbered as a leader in the Philistine army. He would have to go to war with his own country. Miraculously, God changed things in Philistia, saving David from an awful choice:

> And the lords of the Philistines passed on by hundreds, and by thousands: but David and his men passed on in the rearward with Achish. Then said the princes of the Philistines, "What do these Hebrews here?" And Achish said unto the princes of the Philistines, "Is not this David, the servant of Saul the king of Israel, which hath been with me these days, or these years, and I have found no fault in him since he fell unto me unto this day?" And the princes of the Philistines were wroth with him; and the prince of the Philistines said unto him, "Make this fellow return, that he may go again to his place which thou hast appointed him, and let him not go down with us to battle, lest in the battle he be an adversary to us: for wherewith should he reconcile himself unto his master? Should it not be with the heads of these men?" (1 Samuel 29:2–4).

So the Philistine leaders talked their king into removing David from the battle.

You might think that David breathed a sigh of relief, saying a prayer of thanks to the Lord for His intervention. Instead, he lied to Achish, saying he was really sorry he wasn't able to go and fight. Though God had delivered him from all the trouble his lying had caused, David was still telling lies.

THE LESSONS OF DAVID AND SAUL

There are a few lessons we should take away from our study of David and Saul. First is the *plurality of sin*. It's impossible for a man to commit just one sin. One sin leads to another, which leads to another. David made one mistake, then he tried to cover it up, then that lead to another lie, and another, until he was in a real fix—having to fight with the enemy against his own people. We cannot be too careful. We cannot assume we can do one little sin and it will have no impact on our lives. Sin leads the way to sin.

A second lesson we learn from the lives of David and Saul is the *potential of sin*. Here are two men anointed by God, placed into positions of authority, and they are involved in lies, disobedience, murder, theft, and consorting with witches. The potential for sin in each of us is beyond what we can imagine. Most of the men I've known who have fallen did so while walking up the mountain of improbability.

A third lesson has to do with the *power of sin*. Sin has incredibly destructive power. The apostle James says that sin, when it is finished, brings forth death. It was sin that killed Saul. Had he chosen to remain close to God, the result of his life would have been different.

I don't know exactly why God allowed Saul's and David's lives to turn out the way they did. But I know that God was sovereign in all that happened. The difference between the two men can probably be traced to the heart. Saul had a heart for himself. David had a heart for God. Perhaps the reason God extricated David, even though he had become involved in sin, was because David had a heart for God. When we face troubles, it's important to remember that. Saul's heart was hardened, and he would not do what God had called him to do. But David's heart was soft, easily broken over his own sin, and he desired to obey the Lord. Each of us must examine our hearts and remain close to the Lord, if we want to see His joy and purpose in our lives.

APPLICATION

1. What led Saul away from God?

   a. What led David away from God?

   b. What was the difference between the two men?

2. What have you found leads you away from a close relationship with Jesus Christ?

   a. What helps you remain close to Him?

3. How would you describe David's misery?

a. What choices did he have?

b. How did God extricate him from the situation?

4. How would you describe Saul's misery?

a. What choices did he have?

b. Why didn't God extricate Saul as He did David?

5. Why was Saul so afraid when he saw the Philistine army?

a. What does the Lord have to say about divination in Isaiah 8:19–22?

b. What is the meaning of Leviticus 19:26b?

c. Why is divination evil?

6. "The best of us are capable of the worst." Do you agree or disagree with that statement? Why?

a. How can one sin lead to another?

b. What power does sin have, according to James 1:15?

7. In your own words, what are the most important lessons of Saul's life?

a. What lessons should David have learned?

b. What has been the most important thing you've learned in this study?

DID YOU KNOW?

Archaeologists are not exactly sure of the location of biblical Endor, the home of the medium Saul consulted. But the best location seems to be about seven miles southeast of Nazareth—in enemy territory. This may be one of the reasons Saul dressed in a disguise. His willingness to put his life in jeopardy to violate God's commands about mediums and witches shows the depth to which he had fallen. All practices of witchcraft are strictly forbidden by God in Scripture, both for then and for now (Exodus 22:18; Deuteronomy 18:9–14; 1 Samuel 28:3, 9; 2 Kings 23:24; Isaiah 8:19; Acts 19:18–19). Saul should have known better than to inquire of Samuel through a witch, since Samuel had used witchcraft as a benchmark for evil on a prior occasion with Saul (1 Samuel 15:22–23).

Turning Point
Resources
by Dr. David Jeremiah

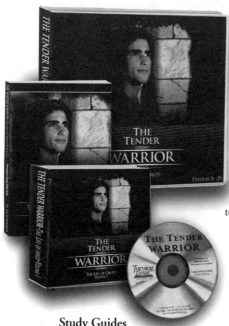

The Tender Warrior:
The Life of David
1 and 2 Samuel

David was a complex man. He was strong and yet weak. Spiritual, but also carnal. A warrior, yet a songwriter. Most of us can relate to these kinds of struggles. Studying the successes and failures of David's life will encourage you to continue to maintain a heart for God. In this series, Dr. Jeremiah tells the beautiful story of a shepherd boy, warrior, and king. His story will encourage you!

Study Guides
Volume 1 TTWSG1 (Can-$14/UK-£6)   **$9**
Volume 2 TTWSG2 (Can-$14/UK-£6)   **$9**
Study Guide Package TTWSGP (Can-$23/UK-£9.50)   *$14.50*

Cassette Albums
Volume 1 TTWAL1 (12 tapes) (Can-$95/UK-£39)   **$60**
Volume 2 TTWAL2 (10 tapes) (Can-$79/UK-£33)   **$50**
Cassette Album Package TTWALP (22 tapes)
          (Can-$128/UK-£57)   *$88*

Compact Disc Albums
Volume 1 TTWAL1CD (12 CDs) (Can-$132/UK-£55)   **$84**
Volume 2 TTWAL2CD (10 CDs) (Can-$110/UK-£45)   **$70**
Compact Disc Album Package TTWALPCD (22 CDs)
          (Can-$195/UK-£81)   *$124*

Turning Point
Resources
by Dr. David Jeremiah

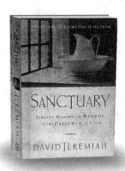

Sanctuary
Finding Moments of Refuge in the Presence of God

Dr. Jeremiah knows the most important time in his day is the time he spends with the Lord. He has been experiencing special times of Bible study, prayer, and worship with God for years, and he wants you to experience intimate moments with the Lord as well. You can now read some of his personal reflections and greatest biblical discoveries in his first-ever devotional book, *Sanctuary.* Bound in a soft, padded cover and filled with 384 pages of calming images and reverent design, *Sanctuary* is the 365-day devotional book you will want for yourself and those you love.

4x6, 384 pages SANHBK (Can-$22 / UK-£9)   **$14**

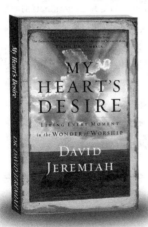

My Heart's Desire
Living Every Moment in the Wonder of Worship

Has your worship lost its wonder? Do you feel distant from God when you're not in church? Worship was never intended to be a Sunday-only event. In *My Heart's Desire,* Dr. Jeremiah explains how to make worship a moment-by-moment reality in your life. Learn to experience the presence of God each and every day through lifestyle worship. And put the wonder back in your walk with God!

Hard Cover Book - 210 pages MHDHBK (Can-$30 / UK-£12.50)   **$19**

ORDER 1-800-947-1993

Turning Point Resources

STUDY GUIDES

All Study Guides are regularly priced at $9
An audiocassette album is also available for each of the following series.
(Sold separately. Individually priced.)

Authentic Christian Life, The
   (I Corinthians, 3 Volumes)
Bend in the Road, A (Psalms)
Celebrate His Love (Christmas)
Christians Have Stress Too
Christ's Death and Resurrection
Escape the Coming Night
   (Revelation, 4 Volumes)
Facing the Giants in Your Life
Family Factor
For Such a Time as This (Esther)
Fruit of the Spirit, The (Galatians)
Gifts from God (Parenting)
Giving to God
God in You (The Holy Spirit)
God Meant It for Good (Joseph, 2 Volumes)
Grace of Giving, The (Stewardship)
Greatest Stories Ever Told, The (Parables)
Handwriting on the Wall (Daniel, 3 Volumes)
Heroes of the Faith (Hebrews)
Home Improvement
How to Be Happy According to Jesus
   (The Beatitudes)
How to Live According to Jesus
   (The Sermon on the Mount, 2 Volumes)
Invasion of Other Gods (New Age)
Investing for Eternity
Issues of the Home and Family
Jesus' Final Warning (Prophecy)

Knowing the God You Worship
Learning to Live by Faith (Abraham,
   2 Volumes)
Living by Faith (Romans, 5 Volumes)
Looking for the Savior (Thessalonians,
   2 Volumes)
Miracles of Christ, The
My Heart's Desire (Worship)
Nation in Crisis, A (Joshua, 2 Volumes)
New Spirituality, The (New Age)
Overcoming Loneliness
People God Uses, The
People Who Met Jesus
Power of Encouragement, The
Power of Love, The
Powerful Principles from Proverbs
Prayer—The Great Adventure
Runaway Prophet—Jonah, The
Ruth, Romance, and Redemption
Seeking Wisdom—Finding Gold
Signs of the Second Coming
Spiritual Warfare
Stewardship Is Lordship
Ten Burning Questions from Psalms
Tender Warrior, The (David, 2 Volumes)
Turning Toward Integrity (James)
Turning Toward Joy (Philippians)
What the Bible Says About Angels
When Wisdom Turns to Foolishness (Solomon)

BOOKS

Bend in the Road, A (Psalms) $19
Escape the Coming Night (Revelation) $13
Gifts from God (Parenting) $19
God in You (The Holy Spirit) $19
Handwriting on the Wall, The (Daniel) $12
Invasion of Other Gods (New Age) $13
Jesus' Final Warning (Prophecy) $19
My Heart's Desire (Worship) $19
Power of Encouragement, The $13

Prayer—The Great Adventure $19
Sanctuary (Daily Devotional) $14
Slaying the Giants in Your Life $19
Stories of Hope from a Bend in the Road $13
Things That Matter, The $10
Turning Toward Integrity (James) $10
Turning Toward Joy (Philippians) $10
What the Bible Says About Angels $13

BOOKLETS

Creative Family Living: 20 Ideas for Christian
   Family Interaction $6.50
Family Turning Points $6.50
Financial Turning Points $6.50
How to Encourage Your Children $2.50
Knowing God by Name $2.50
Living Right! 25 Behaviors of a Christian $6.50
Patriotic Turning Points $6.50

Powerful Prayer Promises $2.50
Prayer for Whosoever, A $2.50
Prophetic Turning Points $6.50
Signs at the Bend in the Road $2.50
Tour of Duty $4.00
Walking Down the Romans Road $2.50
Who I Am in Christ $2.50
Your Greatest Turning Point $2.50

POSTAGE AND HANDLING CHART

For orders	Add
Up to $5.99	$1.50
$6.00-$19.99	$2.50
$20.00-$50.99	$3.50
$51.00-$99.99	$6.00
$100.00 & over	$9.00

If you would like a complete catalog
of resources available from
Turning Point, please call
1-800-947-1993 or write
Turning Point ~ P.O. Box 3838 ~
San Diego, CA 92163-1838.
You can also visit Turning Point at
www.turningpointonline.org